Makers of Modern Cu

Makers of Modern Culture

FIVE TWENTIETH-CENTURY THINKERS

Roland N. Stromberg
The University of Wisconsin
at Milwaukee

HARLAN DAVIDSON, INC.
ARLINGTON HEIGHTS, ILLINOIS 60004

Library of Congress Cataloging-in-Publication Data

Stromberg, Roland N., 1916–
Makers of modern culture : five twentieth century thinkers / by Roland N. Stromberg.
p. cm.
Includes bibliographical references and index.
ISBN 0-88295-875-5
1. Intellectuals—Europe—Biography. 2. Europe—Intellectual life—20th century. I. Title.
CT759.S77 1991
001'.092'24—dc20   90-43701
[B]   CIP

Manufactured in the United States of America
95 94 93 92 91 1 2 3 4 5   MG

Contents

Introduction

THIS presentation of five major twentieth-century thinkers—Sigmund Freud, Albert Einstein, Ludwig Wittgenstein, James Joyce, and Jean-Paul Sartre—seeks to introduce these important and interesting figures to the beginning student. Taken together, they provide an understanding of much of this century's intellectual history. Each of these giants of the written word exerted an influence that affected the entire culture. They came from diverse intellectual and geographic realms, but they all had in common a brilliance and originality of mind.

By discussing the contributions of these five thinkers, I hope to relate something about our contemporary culture and society, and perhaps also something about the nature of creative genius, though this is not the primary purpose. Each chapter includes biographical narrative as well as a discussion of the intellectual achievements of the person. Because each of our subjects was influenced by the immense sea of literature and thought of his day as well as the general history and culture of his era, I have included some background material of this sort. Attempting to make clear how they interacted with the surrounding milieu of ideas, past and present, is a prime objective of this study. As an intellectual historian, I believe the goal of my discipline is to grasp and then describe the totality of mind at some particular moment in time. Comprehending the ideas of this century is a special need for present-day people living in a culture so vast and fragmented that it eludes understanding.

These writers touched on a range of disciplines embracing literature, philosophy, physical science, psychology, and social criticism. My intention, however, is less to address the experts in these respective disciplines than to introduce these thinkers as the authors of books and ideas that deeply affected twentieth-century minds and lives.

There is little need to spend time justifying our choices. The five chosen do not, of course, exhaust the list of possibilities, which is almost endless. Still, all five are acknowledged giants who left a deep imprint on the consciousness of modern times. They all, additionally, were charismatic personalities. And they all had extraordinary range. Freud was far more than a psychologist in the technical sense; indeed he seems, curiously, to have influenced professional psychologists less than writers, critics, and the general public. Einstein was a physicist, Wittgenstein a philosopher, Joyce a novelist, but the scope as well as the impact of all three far transcended these specific domains of achievement. Sartre was the most obviously versatile of the group, at once novelist, playwright, philosopher, political activist, essayist, and editor (also film scriptwriter, biographer, and social theorist.) The greatness of our five subjects lay in their ability to break down barriers of academic specialization. They were all deep and profound thinkers, but they became much more than that.

They were notably international. We have an Irishman and a Frenchman plus three who belonged to the German (or Austrian) cultural world. But of these latter three (who all had a Jewish heritage), one spent most of his career in England, and another lived his final years in the United States. Joyce left his native Ireland to wander about from Italy to Switzerland to France. No doubt significantly, there is an increase in this mobility as the century wears on: the stablest personality in all respects was the oldest, Freud, who never changed residence (until perforce in the last year of his life) or mates. But Freud, like the others, had a global following, and his disciples could be found in all countries. Freud himself, immersed in the European cultural inheritance, was a true product of the West's civilized consciousness. This was true of all our five thinkers. Even the apparently iconoclastic avant-garde figure, James Joyce, actually built on the classical education the Jesuits of Dublin gave him; one cannot imagine his mind without the influence of Dante, Bruno, Vico, and Swift. Sartre too had mastered the Western inheritance before moving to revolutionary frontiers. Revolutions, paradoxically, come out of tradition.

It would seem that the place of birth was of little consequence to any of our group (though it has been argued otherwise); they illustrate the essential unity of a single republic of letters, an international community of knowledge. Joyce, it will be said, cannot be thought of apart from the Dublin he made the scene of his great books; but of course *Ulysses* and *Finnegans Wake* are not really about Dubliners, they are about the human consciousness in general. The artist, unlike the scientist, must have local habitations and names for his ideas, but these can be found anywhere. With his amalgamation of languages and myths Joyce was as universal a scholar as Einstein or Wittgenstein. Likewise, it has been argued that Wittgenstein was distinctively Viennese; the truth in this is trivial.

A special quality of notoriety distinguishes our group. They had charisma as well as talent. It is difficult to tell whether the former resulted from the latter, or vice versa; whether, that is, the glamor was an aura created by the dazzling gifts of intellect, or whether the reputation for brilliance was at least partially the consequence of a flamboyant personality. Einstein and Wittgenstein are examples. While no one doubts that the former was a great scientist, some have argued that he was not in a technical sense the greatest one—not on close inspection either a truly top-flight mathematician or a great experimentalist. Certainly there were many other scientists who worked with equal genius in his field, even some who hit upon the same ideas he did (or very nearly so) yet are not recognized as he is. Einstein had some elusive quality of imagination that set him apart. Was this a genuine gift of the gods or an illusion created by his uncanny personality? Or was it that he simply happened to be in the right place at the right time? As for Ludwig Wittgenstein, his was hardly the only first-class philosophical mind of the century. That he stands out from all the others, as he undeniably does, may be because of his superior imagination, originality, and scope; or it may owe something to the haze of magic that surrounds his persona. In this connection the philosopher Arthur Danto, reviewing a book by a leading philosopher who, immune to the Wittgenstein charm, treated him as a more or less ordinary thinker, remarked that

> There is scarcely a line in either book [Wittgenstein's] that is not dense
> with philosophical excitement, poetry, urgency, and passion.[1]

This excitement is present in all our five; it is what sets them apart from others who were equally as capable.

Some chronological guidance: fifty years separate the birth of the oldest, Freud, from the youngest, Sartre; the others fall in the generation between. That generation was the first modernist one. Freud's first major work coincided exactly with the twentieth century's beginning, but he did not achieve much fame until the 1920s. The astronomical observation that overnight made Einstein an international celebrity in 1919 was followed by the sensational debates of the 1920s about the crisis in science. Joyce's *Ulysses* was a sensation of the same decade. Wittgenstein's first book, the only one he published in his lifetime, appeared in 1922. So, Jean-Paul Sartre apart—and his mind was largely shaped in the 1920s—we have here, it may be objected, an intellectual history of at most the first half of the twentieth century. But what Freud, Einstein, and Joyce started lingered on to shape the rest of the century. Sartre, living until 1980, ranked as the dean of French intellectual life until the end, though in his last years he was blind and ill. The others had long since passed from the scene physically (Freud in 1939, Joyce in 1941, Wittgenstein in 1951, and Einstein in 1955) but their influence remained powerful.

There is a huge body of scholarly and critical literature about these figures that shows no sign of diminishing. Appended to our biographies is a bibliographical essay intended to direct the more curious student, or one interested in doing advanced research, to this literature.

A note on gender: It will doubtless not escape attention that all five of our protagonists were male. The justification for this must be that it was a masculine century. The next one may be different. The twentieth century did have a notable feminine literary and intellectual presence—not that this was so new. Branded by feminists as a classical era of patriarchy, the nineteenth century had also produced a vigorous crop of women writers; the names of George Eliot, the Brontë sisters, Elizabeth Barrett Browning, Christina Rossetti, Harriet Martineau, Annie Besant, and a host of others remind one of the importance of women for Victorian literature and thought. And it would be easy to assemble a gallery of women greats of the twentieth century not far behind our group: say (in the same disciplines of our five) Melanie Klein, Marie Curie, Simone Weil, Virginia Woolf, Simone de Beauvoir. (We will include some discussion of Beauvoir in the Sartre chapter.) But few would claim they were the primary figures. Women's roles had begun to change; through most of the century, however, they did not shift enough to bring women into the universities, the writing and artistic professions, or for that matter the world of bohemia, in the same numbers as men.

But the presence of the other sex haunted and shaped our masculine thinkers in many ways. At the beginning of the century a young Viennese disciple of Friedrich Nietzsche, Otto Weininger, of the same generation as Joyce and Wittgenstein, wrote a brilliant, perturbed book about sexual differences and then at the age of twenty-three committed suicide. It was a symbol for the century. The *Frauenfrage*, the "woman question," loomed early in the century as a profound shaper of character and imagination. All our five thinkers, along with numerous others, fought their way to creativity via the sublimation, as Freud called it, of sexual anguish. At any rate each of them had curious erotic histories, strange relations with the opposite sex. (The least abnormal was the theorist of sexuality, Sigmund Freud.)

Our chapters will not be able to do much more than introduce such questions about the lives, the loves, the motivations, and the genius of these five leaders. What is beyond doubt is that they were all intensely interesting people as well as seminal thinkers and writers. Getting acquainted with them is a first step toward getting acquainted with the history of our century. Examining their lives is also a rich source for understanding human creativity.

[1] *Russell Society Newsletter,* No. 57, February 1988.

FREUD

SIGMUND Freud opened the twentieth century with his greatest work, *The Interpretation of Dreams*. George Bernard Shaw, born in the same year as Freud (1856), wrote perhaps his weightiest play, *Man and Superman*, at this same moment. Bertrand Russell thought that Shaw's influence in Britain was akin to Freud's on the Continent, bringing into discussion once tabooed sexual and family subjects. The German philosopher Edmund Husserl (b. 1857) published his pioneer work on phenomenology also in 1901. Within a few years the novelists Joyce, D. H. Lawrence, Kafka, and Proust were beginning to create a wholly different kind of literature. "Human character changed in 1910," Virginia Woolf once remarked. What exactly was the intellectual revolution suggested by these notable landmarks? Freud drew on and summed up so much of a long development in intellectual history that it is worth responding to that question as a prelude to our discussion of the great Viennese doctor and writer.

Obviously one element of this new zeitgeist was a greater subjectivity. An interest in those largely unexplored realms of the mind that lie buried in the human consciousness was not entirely new; Rousseau and Kant had begun it a hundred years earlier, and to Wordsworth during the Romantic era "the Mind of Man" had been "my haunt, and the main region of my song." Yet this realm was now to be explored with a new intensity, and more systematically. The science of psychology was born in the last decades of the nineteenth century. (William Wundt is credited with setting up the first psychology laboratory in 1879, in Leipzig, where Nietzsche had studied.) The mind was to be studied in the scientific manner rather than the poetic. To be sure, others had tried fumblingly to do this earlier, notably Destutt de Tracy and the so-called Ideologues of the late eighteenth century. But this enterprise had failed. A new frankness contributed to these novel intellectual explorations. One barrier to full exposure of private realms, doubtless the greatest, had been reticence, embarrassment, and fear of breaching taboos. How differently men would behold the world, Byron mused in 1820 (and "how much would novels gain")

> If some Columbus of the moral seas
> Would show mankind their souls' antipodes.

The stanza that follows (*Don Juan*, Canto 14, cii) speaks obscurely of terrible secrets which, "with self-love in the centre," lie in the hearts of even the greatest men. Caesar himself would be ashamed "were things but only call'd by their right name." Byron must have meant more than the banal assertion that people are sinful and hypocritical. He hints at what Nietzsche so brilliantly argued a half century later: virtues are really rooted in vices, i.e., in self-love, self-interest. A few stanzas later, Byron refers to "the sigh supprest/Corroding in the cavern of the heart," which seems a clear anticipation of one of Freud's best known ideas, that repression leads to neurosis.

The great imaginative writers anticipated Freud, as he knew and acknowledged. Shakespeare, Goethe, and Dostoyevsky, he said, "had come closer to the fundamental truths of psychoanalysis than had the physicians." A recent student of Dickens finds something that anticipates Freud in that popular Victorian novelist.[1] They both believed that "the process of socialization transforms the individual by endowing him with an inner faculty of civilization," which Freud called the "superego" and Dickens simply the soul; to most of us it is the conscience. It checks the aggressive instinct by turning it inwards against itself. Freud thought the cost of this internalization was high. Civilization is made possible by a cruel constraint which is the worse for being self-inflicted. One can fight against an external enemy, but "a kind of fighting with oneself" produces—what? Yeats said we make politics out of our quarrels with others, and poetry out of our quarrels with ourselves. In some, unable to be creative, it may produce frustration or self-hate.

"What a potent obstacle to civilization aggressiveness must be, if the defense against it can cause as much unhappiness as aggressiveness itself!" Freud wrote.

In 1838 Dickens attended lectures at London University on mesmerism by John Elliotson, a brilliant professor of medicine, who soon became involved in controversies over this new therapy and was forced to resign his teaching position—anticipating Freud's battles six decades later. ("The Victorians especially feared that sacred taboos about sexual relationships might be transgressed by male operators with their mesmerized female subjects," writes Dickens's biographer Fred Kaplan.) In 1779 Anton Mesmer, a Viennese like Freud, had declared himself the discoverer of "animal magnetism," carried he thought by an invisible fluid, the management of which could achieve marvelous powers over nature, society, and the self. His erroneous theories had a great popularity in the era of the French Revolution. It gradually became evident that no such fluid existed, yet the phenomena of psychological suggestion did appear valid. Dickens discovered that he himself possessed mesmeric or (as the term soon became) hypnotic powers, and during 1844 and 1845 he aroused his wife's extreme jealousy by applying mesmerism at all hours of the day and night to a friend's wife who suffered from muscular contractions and convulsive seizures that were alleviated under hypnotic trance. While she was in the trance, Dickens questioned her about her dreams and nightmares, seeking to learn more about the "phantom" that she said threatened her. Though Dickens developed no theories, the experience certainly reminds us of Freud's.[2]

The great early nineteenth-century French novelist Stendhal in his autobiographical *Vie de Henry Brulard* (Brulard was a disguise, an alter ego) tried to recover the real record of his past in order to "divine what kind of man I have been." But he had to give up before the bottomless well of memory. Each year adds another five feet of memories burying or hopelessly refracting the deeper ones, he noted. Brulard begins to have memories of memories (I remember that I always remembered that, then I remember that I remembered that I remembered . . .) and in this game of mirrors he loses all certainty of recovering earlier recollections. "I do not know what I am," Brulard has to admit. The key to mastering our shifting and complex self is, then, to find a way to recover and to order these buried experiences.

Stendhal (pseudonym of the "real" Henri Beyle) believed that "nowhere else can we come as close to the true as in the novel." Others were saying that we need to do better than this. The imagination, with its sentiment and subjectivity, is slovenly and error-prone. Nineteenth-century scientists hoped to found knowledge on careful experiment and close reasoning. Freud's discoveries are inconceivable without Darwin, whose naturalistic view of human evolution underlies the Freudian outlook. In the wake of Darwin's sensational biological claims, many were applying the evolutionary hypothesis to man's moral and philosophical ideas and his institutions; they are not eternal and unalterable, these thinkers declared, but develop through time, changing in accordance with their aptitude for survival. At this time anthropology and sociology were born as social sciences to study these fascinating processes.[3] More basically, Darwin had introduced a naturalism that came to view matters of the mind and spirit as data to be ascertained and classified in the same way science deals with physical phenomena, that is, as determinate products of natural forces.

The list of contributors to one or another of Freud's theories is a long one. It includes the German philosopher Arthur Schopenhauer as well as Friedrich Nietzsche, whom Schopenhauer influenced and who in turn provided Freud with some key ideas. The electrifying Nietzsche, writing chiefly in the 1880s, pointed out that our motives are often unconscious and unrecognized. We rationalize, failing to understand the real reasons why we did something—perhaps because we do not want to know. The world within is as mysterious as the world without. "We have taken great pains to learn that external things are not as they appear to us. Well! It is the same with the inner world." We are ignorant about ourselves. Again, "we couple the generation of human beings with a bad conscience"; in other words, we feel guilty about sex, and this is a source of problems. "He who thinks he has killed his sensuality is wrong, for his sensuality lives on in an uncanny vampire form, and torments him in hideous disguises." But we can "sublimate," making this sexual energy a source of creativity, of great art. Nietzsche also speculated that dreams may be compensatory, revealing unfulfilled wishes. Here were a host of suggestions, which Carl Jung as well as Freud picked up from Nietzsche.

The nineteenth century is filled with speculations about the meaning of dreams; Freud himself was to serve as the historian of this ancient inquiry. So, too, the "unconscious" was a fashionable term around 1870; its roots may be traced as far back as St. Augustine, but the

Schopenhauer disciple von Hartmann had made it topical in 1869 with his *Philosophy of the Unconscious.* Probably we should give up and say simply that Freud was a product of the entire European intellectual inheritance. Though educated as a physician, he had read deeply in the classics, drawing from them names for psychological phenomena, as everybody knows (Oedipus, Narcissus, Eros). Some have claimed that Freud's Jewish heritage, with its elaborate interpretation of religious texts and commentaries that attempt to provide guidance, was a significant influence on the development of psychoanalysis. Freud's reading extended widely through European literature. He once cited Diderot's "Rameau's Nephew," in which this celebrated eighteenth century *philosophe*, admired by Hegel and Marx, imagines a dialogue between the outer, respectable self and a rude, antisocial rascal who seems to be the alter ego or suppressed self. Diderot even says that this little savage would like to wring his father's neck and go to bed with his mother.

The liberation of sex from earlier widespread taboos, so often associated with Freud, actually predated him or emerged about the same time from many other directions. Another Viennese doctor, Krafft-Ebing, published a famous manual of sexual behavior just about the time Freud began his career (1886). The "new woman" was a familiar term as early as the 1880s. The children of the mid-Victorians, obeying a law of oppugnancy, made a practice of defying the tight morals and high seriousness of their parents. The Edwardian era (roughly the first decade of the twentieth century) featured a new daring in the portrayal of sex and sexual morality. Shaw was joined here by H. G. Wells, Elinor Glyn, John Galsworthy, and others. There were those who were classifiable more directly as sexologists; they included Magnus Hirschfeld and Havelock Ellis.

This "emancipation" was championed by many others besides Freud, even if he was its boldest and most incisive representative. The causes for the questioning of sexual mores went deeper than literary or scientific fashions. The conditions which made social control over personal behavior vulnerable were those of modern urban life, modern economic production, and modern technology. Society was being secularized, government democratized, the economy globalized. People became more mobile, life more subject to often traumatic change. This great transformation of Western society from traditional to modern—a long slow process that was now accelerating—was being described in Freud's generation by a crew of "sociologists," who fumbled for terms to characterize it. Durkheim, Tönnies, Simmel, Max Weber, and others were all trying to analyze and classify this progression from a closed to an open society, from a rural, static one to an urban, dynamic one, with all the concomitant changes in laws, customs, and ways of life. Changes in attitudes toward sex, marriage, and family were just one part of this great transformation. The individual was emancipated from social controls, only to find his or her freedom the source of anxieties as well as exhilarations.

Freud's talent then was to synthesize numerous ideas, some quite unoriginal, indeed almost commonplace, but heretofore rarely treated either systematically or scientifically: dreams, hidden motives, divided selves, unconscious determinants, sexuality and its repression, aggressive instincts or habits, unmentionable urges and wishes. Seldom had these subjects been brought together under the roof of one integrating theory. Theologians and moralists had discussed some of them, poets and novelists had hinted at them, quacks and magicians had trafficked in them, but no one had tied them together intelligently. If Freud failed to complete his science, this is hardly surprising, to say the least; he had taken on a task so difficult that all other intellectual enterprises pale into insignificance beside it. His was a great achievement, and he was hardly being immodest when he compared himself to Copernicus and Darwin as the author of a revolution in basic outlook concerning man's place in the natural world. He did not escape the outrage that had similarly greeted those two earlier challengers to human pretensions. Controversy still pursues the man whom some hail as the decisive genius of our age and others disparage as a mountebank. But the latter charge can scarcely survive a glance at Freud's brilliant career.

Serious, studious, and ambitious, he was top of his class at the Gymnasium he attended and went on to medical school at the distinguished University of Vienna. That after joining the Vienna General Hospital he soon began to specialize in "nervous disorders" was at least partly because this developing area offered opportunities for lucrative practice. He fell in love with and subsequently married Martha Bernays, the only woman in his life. She was from a distinguished Viennese family, which like Freud's, was Jewish (his was scarcely upper-crust, however). There is little in Freud's personality to suggest the revolutionary, except his strong will to power and searching intellectual curiosity, which may of course be found in others than the rebellious. He once described himself as by temperament "a conquistador, an adventurer," and certainly a powerful drive not only to succeed but to innovate, to create and lead a movement, was always evident in Freud. But he was not by nature a rebel in the destructive or antisocial sense, like many of the poets and artists of his era.

Because of his theories, Freud was destined to become known as something of a priest of love, but he disappointed those who came in search of erotic adventures: he was faithful to Martha and a good family man. (Those who would like to overthrow Freud's purity allege an early affair with his wife's sister; the evidence for more than a mild flirtation, however, is far from convincing.) Some interpreters see Freud as a Schopenhauerian pessimist rather than a Nietzschean optimist, regarding the libidinous will or Life Force as more of an affliction than a joy. He did not indulge in the joys of sex, extramaritally at least, and he did not believe civilization could survive unrestrained sexual liberty. Karl Marx collected pornography, but it is hard to imagine Freud doing so. A young lady who managed to seduce Carl Jung evidently failed with Freud.[4]

He apprenticed respectably in Paris with the celebrated Dr. Jean Martin Charcot, a leader in the medical treatment of the insane with a special interest in cases of hysteria. "No other human being has so affected me," Freud said. (Charcot, however, never agreed with Freud's later views; he thought hereditary causes the most important in mental illness.) Freud was well grounded in physical anatomy and general medicine; even so, he came to treat mental illness as a functional, non-physiological matter (but he never thought the physiological side irrelevant). The young doctor was more interested in research than in practice, but he did practice as a physician all his life—no mere armchair theorist was he. Far more than Marx's life, Freud's was an example of *praxis*, the creative interaction of theory and practice. His growing reputation as a specialist in treating mental disorders brought him patients whose case histories he was to make famous. At first Freud collaborated with an older physician, Joseph Breuer, who was content after a while to leave such risky business to the younger man. Breuer coauthored Freud's first book (1895)—*Studies on Hysteria*. On the findings of what some called a too-restricted experimental basis, Freud boldly developed in this book his theories about repression and infantile sexuality and worked out his therapy based on free association and dream interpretation as a means of uncovering material in the unconscious part of the mind. Cases of "hysteria," i.e. ailments or impairments which had no apparent physical cause, could be traced to some painful experience which is pushed into the unconscious and forgotten. Relief comes when the unpleasant memory is retrieved into consciousness, he thought.

In 1897 Freud undertook a self-analysis, stemming from his belief that very early childhood experiences, especially sexual ones, are the key to understanding adult neurotic behavior. "The Oedipus complex is the nucleus of the neuroses." He found sexual love of the mother and jealousy of the father in his own case, he thought, between the ages of two and two-and-a-half. He believed this to be an almost universal experience. The Romantic notion of innocent childhood was slain! The ancient Greek myth of the hero who unknowingly killed his father and married his mother provided Freud, the lover of classical literature, with his colorful name for this psychodrama of infancy.

Freud's great book on *The Interpretation of Dreams* (1900) developed the thesis that dream interpretation is "the royal road to knowledge of the unconscious." Dreams are disguised or distorted desires, and in sleep the guard is down, so there is less resistance to uncovering some buried memory. So, properly construed, dreams may open the road to recovery from neurosis. Needless to say by almost all accounts Freud was a superb analyst: "incisive, sure, bold, possessed of tremendous empathy" (Abraham Kardiner). A great interpreter of dreams! A rare combination of imagination and intellect.

Freud's peculiar genius lay in this mixture of art and science. Bleuler, the notable Swiss psychiatrist, appraised him as more an artist than a scientist; his use of metaphors from literature, his interest in the arts, his powerfully creative pen all suggest this side of him. Yet Freud proclaimed himself a no-nonsense scientist. That he had "no sentimentality at all" (Kardiner) was why he was such a good analyst; a clinical objectivity marked the sessions of analysis, the psychoanalyst turning his back on the patient as he listened. If "transference" occurred, and the patient became too attached to the analyst, as often happened, it was supposed to be firmly resisted. The model of scientific, tough-minded realism, so powerfully preached and exemplified by Darwin and Pasteur, deeply influenced Freud, as it did many others of his generation. He discarded religion, being a somewhat gloomy atheist, and tried not to mix philosophy with psychoanalysis. This position became an issue in his quarrel with Carl Jung, whom he reproached for mystical and irrationalist tendencies. He regarded art as neurotic escape, a retreat into fantasy. Freud never wrote imaginative literature, though he liked to analyze works of art and literature. Most of his thought was published in austere scholarly journals. (The Psychoanalytical Association developed its own network of conferences and journals on the model of the scientific society.) In these ways he was the very model of a modern scientific rationalist and positivist, supposedly casting aside all religious and metaphysical "superstition" to rely only on hard experimental evidence. It is true that the later Freud became more speculative, but he always distanced himself from religion, poetry, and metaphysics.

Freud became a professor at the University of Vienna, a promotion he thought unjustly denied him too long because of prejudice (against his Jewishness as well as against his doctrines), but which he did obtain in 1902. So in addition to a time-consuming practice (psychoanalytic therapy was never renowned for its brevity!) and a growing body of publications, Freud delivered university lectures on Saturday mornings. Listeners commented on their incisiveness and lucidity. After 1902 he began to gather about him a body of disciples, which by 1909 had grown into the International Psychoanalytical Association—in collaboration initially with the young Swiss psychiatrist Carl Jung, who had independently developed ideas similar (or so it appeared at first) to Freud's. From this small nucleus a large worldwide organization gradually grew. The American lectures of Jung and Freud in 1909 contributed notably to the spread of the movement.

Freud's sectarian clannishness, like that of Marx, was a source both of strength and suspicion. Freud was evidently claiming to be the priest of a new cult holding itself apart from the general body of scientific psychology. Einstein (or, to take an example closer to the human studies, Stanley Jevons, the author of a revolution in economics) did not set up a separate organization, but sent his findings to the mainstream scientific community that studied physics (in Jevons's case economics) to be criticized or accepted on their merits. Einstein did not organize an International Relativity Society and insist on a loyalty test for membership, nor did Jevons establish a Marginal Utility cult, but Freud just about did so with psychoanalysis. He was prone to expel deviating disciples in a way that reminds us more of the Communist party than a scientific society. The history of the IPA is littered with such quarrels and schisms and ostracisms. Reenacting the oedipal drama of revolt against the father, nearly every one of Freud's early disciples eventually broke away to set up his own shop amid emotional recriminations. Psychoanalysis, in brief, showed features of the religious cult even as it posed as a scientific movement. Freud's famous break with Jung was handled in a highly emotional way by both men, suggestive either of their immaturity or intense religious commitment. Freud fainted on a couple of occasions and the two exchanged insults impugning each other's integrity and sanity. When Otto Rank, a long-time Freud associate, deviated from standard doctrine the Freud circle labelled him psychotic. Lionel Trilling, drawing from Ernest Jones's hagiographic biography of Freud (long regarded as canonical among followers), wrote in 1955 that Rank had died insane, whereas in fact between 1925 and 1939 he had had a successful career in New York. There are other examples.

On the other hand, Freud could be remarkably undogmatic at times. He remained sceptical of political nostrums, "refusing," as he said, "to play the prophet." His late speculations on human destiny, *Civilization and Its Discontents* and *The Future of an Illusion* are keenly perceptive but deeply disillusioned. He scornfully rejected the crutch of religion, calling it the "collective neurosis," and unlike Jung refused to honor the great human myths which inhabit the unconscious; instead, Freud believed that man had to replace this archaic "id" element with "ego" or rational control. But man is so aggressive and antisocial by nature that if we repress the id we condemn ourselves to neurosis. The collective neurosis may be the best we can get in an imperfect world, pending the victory of a science advancing with painful slowness. In such moods Freud denies that he has any utopia to offer, since he himself has only barely begun the long march of science.

His book *Totem and Taboo*, published in 1913, nevertheless presented a thesis so fanciful it was difficult for earthbound anthropologists to take it seriously. The view that human beings originally all lived in groups consisting of an older male who appropriated all the females while intimidating or disposing of the younger males was evidently derived from James Frazer's popular book *The Golden Bough* along with some hints from Darwin. In a primal act of rebellion the young men finally killed (and ate) the father-tyrant. Thereafter, in an attempt to prevent repetition of so terrible a crime, they erected totem and incest taboos. Thus the Oedipus complex belongs to society as a whole as well as to each individual, who recapitulates in his personal development the history of the race. Freud here accepts Carl Jung's view of a collective unconscious (everyone preserves in his or her mind the memory of great historic events belonging to the human race as a whole and also to particular ethnic segments of it). Although imaginative and provocative, this essay in speculative history was so little buttressed by factual evidence that it seemed itself to be more myth than science.

For the creative writer and artist, Freud opened up hitherto taboo themes of sexuality including perversions, incest, and homosexuality, and he had given them the ingredients of a new tragic drama: dark, unconscious forces struggling with those of rational, social control. Again, it is difficult to separate Freud from a host of others who pioneered this development at almost the same time. Before D. H. Lawrence had read Freud, he published in 1913 his great oedipal novel *Sons and Lovers*, about a young man struggling to release himself from the love of his mother that inhibits his relations with other women. Proust's mammoth novel of recollection, *À la recherche du temps perdu* (*In Search of Lost Time*, often translated as *Remembrance of Things Past*), is like Freudian therapy in its search for healing self-knowledge via uncovered childhood memories. But Proust evidently owed nothing to Freud. James Joyce as well as Franz Kafka are different stories; still, Joyce's debts to many others are as great as they are to Freud and Jung. There is no doubt that Freud's influence in the 1920s strongly reinforced the modernist literary and artistic renaissance, which coincided with the major reception of his doctrine. Yet he himself never liked modernist art! Surrealist painters like Max Ernst and Salvador Dali, who regarded him as their master, aroused in him only incomprehension and faint disgust. Earlier, Arthur Schnitzler, a fellow Viennese physician (who shared with Freud an interest in psychology and made it a theme in his stories and plays) and the Symbolist poet Hoffmansthal thought Freud rather mediocre because he was too systematic. His temperament, after all, was profoundly conservative and antimodernist in many ways.

Again, in the 1920s when he had become a household word (every schoolboy, as Macaulay might have said, had heard of the libido), Freud reaffirmed his old-fashioned Victorian atheism (*The Future of an Illusion*) at a time when the "return to religion" movement was using him as a source. Had he not shown the dark forces of evil lurking in human nature, revealed the tragic predicament of humanity? He had, indeed, turned more pessimistic. The Great War of 1914–18 (which he enthusiastically supported, initially at least, giving "all his libido to Austria-Hungary") convinced him that men are incurably aggressive. "There are present in all men destructive, anti-social and anti-cultural trends." Who can doubt it, looking at the picture of human behavior that unfolded in the Great War and that still unfolds daily in the newspapers? It was after 1920 that Freud fully developed his famous concept of the id (taken from Nietzsche's "Das Es," the "it," by way of Georg Groddeck; it is rendered in the English translations of Freud by the Latin word for "it.") The id is Nietzsche's Dionysian will, a seething energy that is a potential source of creativity but must be disciplined. It is chaotic, aggressive, instinctual. It can lead to drunkenness or rape or murder if not "sublimated" or repressed. The unconscious contains not only the id force but the superego, the force of repression internalized as conscience or obedience to authority, a sense of guilt when we commit some selfish, pleasurable act. Carl Jung, who frankly embraced the need for religion, said Freud had smuggled Jehovah back in, disguised as the superego. ("Recognized or not, the god is present" was the meaning of the Latin slogan Jung emblazoned on the door of his house.)

The ego, the conscious self, is torn between these two forces and cannot satisfy them both. Freud doubtless thought of Plato's image of the soul as charioteer trying to drive the two horses of passion and intellect.[5] Man's double nature was almost a truism, which both Goethe and Nietzsche reaffirmed in the nineteenth century. One of Freud's contemporaries, Ludwig Klages, in 1910 wrote a well-known book about "the mind as the enemy of the soul." To allow superego (religion) full sway, Freud declared, would condemn us to neurosis from frustrations. He did worry about what the masses might do if prematurely deprived of religion because it is in some ways a helpful illusion, but as civilization advances reason subverts religion, and this is not to be resisted. The scientific reason that can eventually teach us to have social control without neurosis depends on this advance. Again, Nietzsche—whom Freud said he tried not to read because he found there the same ideas in another kind of discourse—had made the point: we are all neurotic today, the lonely man is eaten up by his solitude, the man who joins the crowd is eaten by others: take your choice of cannibals.

A deviant disciple, Karen Horney, rebelled at Freud's pessimism: "What is there to hope and strive for?" Freud's answer, obviously, was "the slow advance of reason," but it was a fairly faint hope. That mankind is "a wolfpack, simply a wolfpack," was confirmed by the advance of Nazism in Germany after 1930 of course. Freud refused to accept the easy utopia of the socialists or Communists; the problem of human aggression and neurosis is not simply a matter of private property, but arises under any social order or form of government. In the 1920s such disabused scepticism well suited the "new spirit" of the fashionable "lost generation" sophisticates, those who joined Fitzgerald and Hemingway at Paris bars to celebrate the decline of the West with cocktails and adultery—though Freud shared few of their sentiments.

So Freud became famous: "I am considered a celebrity," he marvelled. Yet despite his imperious will there was little arrogance in the man. His Olympian dignity scorned such pretensions. The number of professional psychoanalysts multiplied in American cities, not entirely to the gratification of Freud, whose essentially aristocratic personality had judged the United States "a great mistake." His cherished daughter Anna found a notable career "treating naughty American children," while the great and near-great brought their own egos to the sage of Vienna. But by this time he was afflicted with a cancer of the jaw which necessitated numerous painful operations. This did not much slow his literary output nor end his medical practice, even in the last year of his life when he was driven from Austria by Hitler's Brown Shirts.

By which time, Auden could write, in his poem in Freud's memory, that

> To us he is no more a person
> Now but a whole climate of opinion.

"He quietly surrounds all our habits of growth," the poet added. Freud doubtless got credit for more influence than he personally deserved. He became a shorthand word for a whole climate of opinion, like Newton, Darwin, and Marx. In some ways, there were even mistakes in this equation of Freud with an allegedly Freudian zeitgeist. Popularly, at least, Freud meant emancipation from conventional sexual morality. The credo "down repression! up libido!" still seems to be the outlook of countless "sex therapists." But, as we know, Freud was not actually much of an advocate of the sexual revolution. He had indeed dared to treat scientifically subjects once reserved for bachelor parties or gutter literature, but so had others. He had, in a sense, legitimized abnormal sexual feelings and practices, by arguing that they are not abnormal at all. Incest and homosexuality, for example, far from being degenerative diseases, as was once commonly thought, can emerge logically from family environments. The male child's erotic attachment to his mother, jealousy of his father, and guilty fears about these feelings, Freud thought, happen or can happen to almost anyone, deriving from typical family situations. Everyone passes through oral and anal phases of sexual pleasure during which some become "fixated." Freud may be credited or faulted for thus encouraging acceptance, as it were, of things once thought vicious, depraved, or physically aberrant.

The clinical study of sex that began before Freud continued after him in the hands of others; it would have happened with or without Freud's discoveries. The Kinseys and Masters and Johnsons, we can hardly doubt, would have struck Freud as rather vulgar, with their cathode-wired copulating couples recording vibrations on a chart. Sex education might have appalled him as much as it did D. H. Lawrence, a true "priest of love" who did not wish to desacralize sex. Freud shared the fear that removing all illusions from sex would destroy love. "In times during which no obstacles to sexual satisfaction existed," he wrote, "love became worthless, and life became empty." Our contemporary sexual sybaritism often is a desperately unhappy trap.

There is an aristocratic subtlety about Freud's methods, implicit in those long, involved analyses that clear up (or perhaps do not clear up[6]) problems of some usually upper-class neurotic. Freudian therapy assumes a good deal of education in the patient, likewise a highly developed conscience, able to feel guilt or shame so deeply as to repress it, not to speak of a substantial income able to absorb the analyst's large bill. To suppose that classical psychoanalysis provides any solution to the massive problem of mental illness today (when statistics indicate that between 10 and 15 percent of the populace in western Europe and the United States at some time need psychiatric help) is laughable, and of course the Freudian method is scarcely used at all by harried psychiatrists dealing in the mass market.[7] Psychoanalysis was more like a form of civilized discourse between wealthy (mostly Jewish, at first) Europeans in the decadence of a rich culture. Even in the United States, where it became a flourishing profession, psychoanalysis was confined largely to a well-off civilized minority.[8] It has been called a religious cult, an intellectual fashion, an ideology for sophisticated postmoderns.

It seems rather beside the point, then, for critics to cry that psychoanalytic treatment usually fails (does any mental therapy fully succeed?), and that it is not "scientific." Professional, academic psychologists (an earthbound crew, Freud would doubtless have thought) have said these things vociferously and copiously. To be sure, the chorus is a bit dissonant. Adverse judgments on Freud's thought, such as "bears no relationship to objective knowledge of the mind," "a mass delusion," "one of the saddest and strangest landmarks in the history of twentieth century thought," come from august professorial sources, but so do estimations such as "far too much has been verified to reject all of Freudian theory," and "parts of the oedipal theory are well affirmed." Rare and rather quaint now is uncritical acceptance of Freud as a scientist who "discovered a whole group of general laws, each valid, each . . . fundamental" (Von Treslar). A group of centrists wants to say that Freud's theories were perhaps valid for a specific time and place, but not universally so (with which he would have vigorously disagreed); or "even when his hypotheses were wrong they proved to be fruitfully stimulating." Or maybe "a solid foundation upon which the building is still being constructed" (Reuben Fine). We may be reminded that Freud did not in fact offer just one theory, but at least six, not necessarily interdependent. We do not any longer see "Freudianism" as a single systematic entity; it is the sum of a remarkably rich and fertile intellect, perhaps as often quirkily wrong as brilliantly right, but always stimulating.

In general, though, we have to grant the point that Freud's main ideas, including the Oedipus complex, repression, and the unconscious, are unproven and unproveable. Does this mean necessarily untrue? They represent essentially a poetic, metaphoric, mythic interpretation. Does this much matter? Some, including Wittgenstein, might argue that this is true of all sciences, especially the behavioral ones.

What no one questions, though some deplore, is Freud's mighty cultural influence. He "revolutionized the thought, the lives, and the imagination of age"; "you cannot open a novel, read a history or biography, discuss a painting or sculpture" without encountering Freud. "Freud's impact on the arts defies description." As a tool of interpretation in biography and history, Freudian concepts have had an equal or greater influence. Still, today's psychobiographer or psychohistorian will seldom use undiluted, pristine Freud, of course. Other schools, some offshoots of his, have added insights or shifted Freud's stress; the seminal influence however was clearly from him. Erikson, Klein, Fairbairn, Kohut, and a score of others grabbed at the master's torch and used its fire to light their own.

Each of the other great schools of twentieth-century thought has had its dialogue with Freud, offering criticisms and emendations, perhaps attempting a synthesis. Each of the figures treated in our subsequent chapters interacts with Freud. Jean-Paul Sartre, who wrote the script for a film about him, helped create an existentialist psychology that faulted the pseudoscientism and materialism of the Freudian terminology. Ludwig Wittgenstein, who ignored psychology until he discovered Freud about 1919 and found "here was someone who had something to say," thought Freudianism "a powerful mythology," more speculation than science and often overly schematic. Those who agreed with Wittgenstein in stressing the linguistic dimension revised Freud to allow for the influence on the mind, even the unconscious mind, of language's deep structures.

There were some between the World Wars who sought to combine the two most fashionable ideologies of the era, Freudianism and Marxism. It was not easy to do. Freud was as suspicious of socialist attempts to change human nature as Marxists were of his assertion that no social order could solve the ultimate human dilemma of id and superego. In trying to harmonize them, Wilhelm Reich managed to get himself ejected from both the Communist party and the International Psychoanalytic Association. Stalin thought Freudianism dangerously subversive. Each dogma tried to deconstruct the other: social revolutionaries could be reduced to abnormal psychological types (symbolically slaying their fathers), or psychiatrists shown to be products of a decaying bourgeois society.

Some leftists accused Freudianism (along with other kinds of psychiatry) of upholding the status quo. The discontented are diagnosed as maladjusted and taught to adapt to the established order of things. One could just as well say, however, that only by learning to interact fruitfully with others can proponents of social change hope to succeed. The psychically whole person can be creative in whatever direction he or she chooses. Psychoanalysis, like other social or behavioral sciences, is normatively neutral.

Though a surprising number of Freud's closest friends and disciples were women (one could mention among others his own daughter Anna, Princess Marie Bonaparte, Karen Horney, Melanie Klein, Helene Deutsch, Lou Andreas-Salome), he was subsequently to be criticized severely by feminists. Classical Freudians, noting the failure of the female to participate in the great Oedipal drama (the comparable jealousy of her mother by a girl they considered not so strong a force), found here an explanation for woman's allegedly weaker creative power. Envying the male's sexual organ, she learns to think of herself as inferior. Freud's own life reflected a belief in the traditional role of woman as wife and mother, staying in the home. It is true that, moving with the times, he had changed somewhat by 1932. Still, most feminists placed him well inside the camp of male chauvinists. Yet they might reflect that no one had done more to focus attention on the issues to which feminists addressed themselves: how sex roles are defined, how sexual oppression and repression take place, how discontented and unfulfilled individuals may conquer their neuroses to become creative and happy. And in fact some feminists have found Freud fascinating, even undergoing analysis and becoming converts. (Reactionary males might detect here an example of a female tendency, noticed by Freud, to desire that which they detest.)

Perhaps the most basic change in human perspectives that Freud helped bring about was revealed to his beloved daughter Anna—the only one of his six children who carried on his work—in a conversation which she recalled from about her fourteenth year. "You see those houses with their lovely façades?" he asked her. "Things are not necessarily so lovely behind the façades. And so it is with human beings too." Some have always felt hostile to psychoanalysts for peering behind the drawn curtains into the secrets of the soul, scandalous though these may be. Or to their insistence that things are never what they seem, deceit is everywhere, and that we must question every alleged motive. It is simple-minded and unsubtle, actually, to apply this formula in a doggedly mechanical way. Human nature slips through the net of any one formula.

But if Thoreau was right in thinking that most people lead lives of quiet desperation, if human beings have been unhappy without knowing why, the remedy may lie in daring to be ruthlessly honest, exposing heretofore unmentionable secrets of human passions and desires. In the last analysis the Freudian revolution, for better or worse, has torn aside the veils to make us look at many things that are shocking, even repulsive, yet essential to the human condition, in the hope that we might ameliorate the suffering and cruelty that are a product of their concealment.

Virginia Woolf's husband, Leonard, met Freud in early 1939, his last year of life, after the Nazi absorption of Austria had forced the great psychiatrist to flee from the Vienna he had lived and worked in virtually all his life. "Nearly all famous men are disappointing," Woolf had thought—either bores or ciphers. Freud, he discovered, was neither: "he had an aura not of fame but of greatness." By that time *Der Fuehrer* had personally presided at a special burning of Freud's books in Vienna, to which Gustav Klimt's paintings were added. (Einstein had already been consigned to the Hitlerite flames.) Greatness or not, Freud's fame was assured, as much by his foes as his friends.

The apartment in Vienna in which he lived and worked for so many years has now become a shrine. But Freud's ashes, along with those of his wife and lifelong companion Martha, lie in Golders Green crematorium in London. His daughter Anna ran a nursery which cared for homeless children in London during World War II, later converting it into a famous clinic for the study of child psychology. She engaged in a celebrated conflict with Melanie Klein, one of Freud's most brilliant disciples, who like almost all of them decided his precepts needed revision. Anna defended the citadels of orthodoxy almost alone. The disciples quarreled and fought with each other constantly, like sibling rivals in a household. This rather unseemly squabbling may tell us much about this substitute religion disguised as a science. That we can find interpretations of Freudianism that formerly did not exist is a tribute to the force of Freud's thought. His controversial ideas have haunted the twentieth century.

The human personality is the most complex system known. No one theory can encompass it. The idioms in which we talk about it are numerous. At one time people spoke of sin, redemption, salvation, the soul, grace, and faith. With the decline of Christian and Judaic theology, a new "scientific" worldview emerged. But scientific reason has yet to decipher the human personality. Psychology today is a vast, indispensable but confused realm. Biomedical approaches (not necessarily incompatible with Freud, who believed that there was a physical side to mental well-being[9]) compete with functional psychologies. Freud and his offshoots stand above all the rest; theirs is the most significant and most interesting attempt to supply modern humanity with a vocabulary to describe the human personality, its vagaries and ailments, its creative powers and its failures.

Notes

[1] Myron Magnet, *Dickens and the Social Order* (1985), pp. 94–95.

[2] Similarly Rosemary Sumner, in *Thomas Hardy: Psychological Novelist* (1981), argues that Hardy anticipated Freud. One wonders if the same case could not be made for every great creative writer.

[3] In 1987 a Freud manuscript of 1915 was discovered. Titled "A Phylogenetic Fantasy," it sketched an evolutionary approach to psychiatry. What we now call mental disorders, Freud speculated, may have been helpful to the survival of the human species in earlier stages of development. But he dropped the idea.

[4] See A. Carotenuto, *A Secret Symmetry: Sabina Spielrein between Freud and Jung* (1982).

[5] Cf. Gerasimos Santas, *Plato and Freud: Two Theories of Love* (1988). A. W. Price, reviewing this book in TLS (formerly known as the *Times Literary Supplement*) (Nov. 4–10, 1988) thinks Plato and Freud were more alike than Santas suggests.

[6] The "Wolf Man," perhaps Freud's most famous case, was a rich, sensitive Russian who wandered from analyst to analyst almost as if he had made it his career to be neurotic, and cannot be said to have ever been "cured." "Anna O.," another key Freud patient, eventually cured herself by finding a fruitful career in social work.

[7] What they do use is harder to say. There are many schools of psychiatry that have some tendency to say each individual case is different and that there is no acceptable theory. The multiplication and constant revision of mental disorders in the classification manual has been a scandal of the last few decades.

[8] In 1977 the International Psychoanalytic Association had over 4,000 members, of whom half resided in the United States. The large American membership no doubt reflected the heavy migration of Jewish intellectuals and professionals who fled Central Europe to escape Nazism.

[9] For a recent argument that physicalist perspectives are by no means inconsistent with psychoanalytic, see among others Morton F. Reiser, *Mind, Brain, Body: Toward a Convergence of Psychoanalysis and Neurobiology* (1985).

EINSTEIN

"I SPENT two hours chattering away with Einstein," Freud wrote in a 1927 letter. "He is merry, self-assured, and amiable. He understands as much of psychology as I do of physics, and so we had a very good talk." It would be interesting to know what they talked about. It was a time of extraordinary apotheosis for both men, who had become joint symbols of the "new spirit" of the restless, iconoclastic 1920s. Einstein at that time was debating with critics at the famous Solvay conference, a key moment in the drama of his earth-shattering ideas. Later Freud and Einstein would collaborate (at a distance) in a book on a subject neither one knew much about—war; about the future of peace Einstein was cheerfully optimistic while Freud was deeply pessimistic.

The criticism that Freud's theories lacked the support of empirical evidence may seem less cogent when we consider the speculative nature of physics in the age of Einstein. About 1930, scientists began to tell us that some ten or twenty billion years ago the entire universe was an incredibly hot and incredibly heavy object no larger than a baseball, which for some reason then began to expand with the speed of light and has been doing so ever since. No one, needless to say, ever saw this "primeval egg," just as no one sees particles which live less than a billionth of a second and occupy no space at all but which, we are assured today, really do exist. Likewise the existence of black holes and quasars are inferences from evidence, not directly observed properties. Modern science is not empirical if that means simply based on sense experience.

It was in fact never so; Kepler and Galileo defied common-sense evidence in their day as much as Planck and Einstein did in this century. Einstein encountered as much scepticism as Freud had because he allegedly offered mere speculative theory without observed evidence. There is an account of a Göttingen professor stalking out of an Einstein lecture around 1914, muttering "bloody nonsense!" Rutherford, the great British experimental physicist, thought Einstein was making up mathematical fantasies without any solid factual basis.

Einstein, the rebel who shocked the world by challenging time-honored views on space, time, and gravity in 1905, had been a complete outsider, a 26-year-old patent office clerk holding informal seminars with a few young friends in his little apartment. He subsequently rebelled against his own rebellion, as it were—he broke with the majority of new-era scientists in the 1920s, the younger men who were his own disciples, and went an increasingly lonely way in his later years. No doubt this was because of his surpassing genius, and yet Einstein in some ways was not an unusually brilliant scientist. (Brilliant, yes, but there were many such; why was Einstein unique?) He was not much of a laboratory experimenter and as a mathematician his gifts were evidently not of the very highest order. What he excelled in was imagination, the imagination to conceive and visualize theories and invent hypotheses. And this daring imagination was surely related to his nonconformist temperament.

Einstein once said there was "something for psychoanalysis" in his personality. He spoke of his indifference to human relations; he felt no emotion at the death of his second wife. His first marriage had ended in divorce; one of his two children, like Joyce's, became a mental case. Einstein's first wife was a fellow physicist who apparently helped him in his work, but he repaid her with little credit or affection, so at least it has been claimed.[1] The second marriage, to a cousin, was totally unromantic. As an adolescent Albert had been something of a problem, and his classmates at the Zurich technical college he attended considered him rude and arrogant. One reason for his failure to secure an academic appointment early on, despite his evident genius, seems to have been this social awkwardness. Einstein had a rebellious, somewhat maladjusted personality—quite in contrast to Freud, the model student and stable family man. The affable, endearing sage whom the world came to love in his later years still maintained some eccentric habits such as not wearing socks that matched. He showed a propensity for far-out political causes. Einstein had childlike characteristics, beyond even the "absent-minded professor" standard.

His early life was less rooted than Freud's, though both shared the misfortune of having somewhat feckless fathers, as did Joyce. The family moved about in southern Germany and then to northern Italy, while Albert went to Switzerland to attend the technical college in Zurich, after failing the entrance examination the first time. It is often said that Albert suffered the handicap of dyslexia as a child, though this is uncertain, but it is plausible that such a reading disability might have pushed him toward mathematics, which he said saved him (Bertrand Russell had the same experience). Perhaps reflecting on his own life, in 1918 Einstein remarked that we construct a view of the cosmos "in order to find in this way the peace and security that we cannot find within the all-too-narrow realm of swirling personal experience."

Before Einstein became spectacularly famous, his special relativity theory, propounded in 1905 in one of his articles, had slowly received enough recognition to earn him an academic appointment at Zurich University in 1910. (The University of Bern turned him down for a faculty position in 1908!) Before he hit upon relativity we find Einstein, like Freud, making some false starts in his quest for something to make him famous. During 1911–12 he went for eighteen months to Prague, where he encountered Zionism (could he have met Franz Kafka?), after which he was brought to the University of Berlin with Max Planck's aid. By now he was working on his so-called general relativity theory, involving a stunning revision of Newton's time-honored law of gravity, and it was this that encountered the most scepticism. Observations made during the solar eclipse of 1919, which captured world-wide attention, appeared to confirm his theory and usher in a new epoch of intellectual history. "The very fabric of the physical universe" had changed.

The renewal of interest in physics as a main arena of controversy was surprising to many. According to one version of the evolution of human thought, the struggle with nature had occupied the first stage, the development of social science the second stage, and the last frontier was the world within the mind. Galileo and Newton were the first heroes, Marx and Darwin the second, Freud and Jung came last. Obviously this model greatly oversimplified things, yet had not physics yielded up all its essential secrets in the great Scientific Revolution of the seventeenth century? Only the details remained to be filled in; the Newtonian foundations stood for all time, the most majestic of human edifices: magnificent, precise, comprehensive. Science meant certainty and immutability. Its laws were clear and perfect. Now, bewilderingly, it seemed that Newton had been incomplete if not wrong, and his whole framework of conclusions, which had constituted the intellectual moorings of Western man for two centuries, required drastic revision. Its very premises—"force" operating on "matter" (the smallest unit being the "atom") through "space" and "time"—were called into question.

Albert Einstein, of course, no less than Sigmund Freud, owed a debt to the work of predecessors. Like Freud he worked with surpassing genius to synthesize quantities of data which had been accumulating for decades in different corners of the scientific mansion, data that called for integration around some new theory. Since about 1885, a host of unassimilated findings and observations had been flowing in from different quarters, leading to considerable confusion among the growing community of scientists. Among those who would fire the young Einstein's eager mind were James Clerk Maxwell, Ernst Mach, M. and Mme. Curie, Henri Poincaré, Max Planck, Hertz and Helmholtz and Lorentz—indeed too many to mention. International societies including Scottish, French, Polish, German, Dutch, and Austrian scientists as well as English, American, Danish, Italian, Russian and already even Japanese representatives were meeting together in conferences and publishing ideas in scientific periodicals. The worldwide exchange of information has been seen as the most notable cause of this new scientific revolution.

This "bewildering array of data" facing the physicist in 1900, just as Einstein arrived on the scene, included the electromagnetic spectrum, radioactivity, X-rays, and the wave theory of light. In 1860, the last of these was thought to have been proven beyond doubt by experiment. At that time it was thought that light evidently required a medium, an "ether," to propagate its waves. Yet the Michelson-Morley experiments of the 1880s seemed puzzlingly to show that no space-substance of this sort existed, for the speed of light is the same whether travelling on the moving earth or not. Another startling find concerned electromagnetics. In 1897, at the famous Cavendish Laboratory of Cambridge University, J. J. Thomson, repeating an experiment of the brilliant but short-lived German Heinrich Hertz, discovered "electrons." A few years later at Cavendish, Ernest Rutherford found that electronic particles can pass right through atoms; these allegedly smallest units of matter (the word atom means "not divisible into anything smaller") were evidently largely hollow shells, containing a nucleus surrounded by negative electrical charges. The atom was not, as Rutherford said he had been brought up to believe (so had everyone else) "a nice hard fellow"—Newton's "solid, massy, hard, impenetrable" particle.

Thus began the long and puzzling quest to find the internal components of the atom (if such an entity existed as more than a verbal abstraction) and their principles of motion, evidently totally different from those of ordinary matter regulated by the classical mechanics. Meanwhile the great Max Planck, working in the area of thermal physics, discovered that heated bodies emit energy discontinuously, in spurts, thus also violating one of Newton's laws of motion. The constant number that Planck found to be the ratio between energy and frequency of radiation was later applied in atomic physics to relations between the mass, velocity, and wave length of electrons, it having become necessary to consider electrons as being both waves and particles.

All of this, and more matter for puzzlement[2] will perhaps not be readily understood even today by the average person, though this knowledge has become elementary to physicists. These discoveries added up to a profound revolution in science which called into question laws thought to be settled by scientists in the seventeenth, eighteenth, and earlier nineteenth centuries. Around 1900 a number of thinkers asked what it all meant and proposed new principles of basic science. Ernst Mach, one of Einstein's early heroes, questioned the legitimacy of terms like atom, electron, and ether. According to Loyd Swenson, the Austrian philosopher and physicist Mach "used critical philosophy to try to strip away as much theory and as many primitive concepts as possible in favor of metrical and mathematical operations." This wariness about words as possible traps had begun to appear in Europe, especially among Viennese philosophers. Only data perceived by the senses, after all, are there. The concepts we make out of these observations (converting, for example, some markings on a plate into "electrons") are manufactured in the mind. Thus we endow them with a pseudo-reality, and conceal or distort the true reality.

Mach included Newtonian absolute time and space in his attack on physically meaningless terms. Relativity in the sense of there being nothing fixed as a standard of measurement was known before Einstein; his contribution was to draw out its startling physical implications. Around 1903 Einstein's little circle in Bern was discussing Poincaré's *Science and Hypothesis*, published the previous year, which supported Mach in pointing out that concepts such as "ether" (which had become a puzzling scientific problem) are only tools of thought, convenient hypotheses, not to be confused with external objective reality. The French mathematician was also aware of relativity. If space and time are not fixed objective realities but only organizing principles in our heads, what implications does this have?

The dismantling of one-time certainties had gone on also in the sacred domain of mathematics. The non-Euclidean geometry explored by Lobachewski, Riemann, and Gauss showed that other systems could be created, based on different postulates (curved rather than straight lines), equally consistent internally—and, as it happened, equally applicable to observations in the physical world. The curved or hyperbolic geometries that earlier had seemed only interesting games turned out to fit the universe of Planck and Einstein better than that of Euclid. Mathematics, like language (of which perhaps it was only a branch), seemed to be not a mirror of nature but an invention telling us more about the human mind than about physical nature.

Einstein's four great immediate predecessors were Mach, Poincaré, Planck, and Lorentz. In particular the relationship between Planck and Einstein was to be long and involved. In a paper of 1905 that he regarded as the most important of the three published that year, Einstein picked up the still obscure "quantum" theory of the older German physicist, dating from 1899–1900, and gave it greater notoriety. Planck in turn was an early and enthusiastic supporter of Einstein, though he did not initially accept all of Einstein's conclusions, especially those about light.

H. A. Lorentz, the prominent Dutch scientist who also became a close, lifelong friend of Albert's, had proposed a solution to the riddle left by the Michelson-Morley experiments. They had shown that the speed of light remains the same regardless of whether it is carried or not on a moving body (the earth in this case). You might as a rough analogy imagine that you got on one of those conveyor belts that speed up walkers in an airport, and it was found that, inexplicably, your speed remained the same whether you were walking on it or not! Lorentz supplied a mathematical formula to allow for this factor, which slightly shortened time in the earth's region; Lorentz said he never imagined there was more than one kind of time and considered his transformation equation "only a heuristic working hypothesis." Poincaré called it fudging. Continuing the analogy with the conveyor, we might say that Lorentz asked us to assume the walker becomes a little smaller, taking shorter steps when he gets on the belt, but did not explain the reasons for this phenomenon.

By 1905 Einstein's answer was that there is in fact no general time, there are only local times. Before it had been assumed that if there are clocks which may, in error, show different times, somewhere there is an official clock that gives *the* correct time. In Einstein's universe there is no such clock. To apply this finding to a common analogy, the clocks, say, in a university classroom might show different times, and each would be correct for that room. We would ask in vain for the right time for everybody all over the campus. The best we could do would be to supply a formula that allowed for distance between buildings. Einstein explained that this is so because there is no absolute measuring rod except the speed of light and this, as the ultimate speed, is invariable, rather like a yardstick that gave the same answer regardless of what it measured. Space and time do not exist as such, since there is nothing (like the "ether," a something-space, a background curtain) for them to occupy. They are simply the byproducts of objects and events. Pressed by busy and ignorant journalists for a quick summary of relativity, Einstein later was accustomed to say, "Before me it was thought that if everything was taken out of the universe, space and time would remain. I showed that if everything was taken out, nothing would remain."

It is also more useful to think of space and time as interrelated, interchangeable, really a single entity, space-time. "From now on," declared Hermann Minkowski, Einstein's Zurich professor and early proponent in 1908, "space by itself and time by itself must sink into the shadows, while only a union of the two is valid." (Minkowski died, much before his time, the next year.) If two events happen in different places, you cannot say, as was always supposed, that they are separated by so many miles and so many minutes (at any given rate of speed). Different observers, accurately, will reach different conclusions about the distances and time between the events. An event on earth, for example, that one observer reports as happening simultaneously with one on Mars will seem to an observer travelling in another part of the cosmos to have happened after it, and to still another observer to have preceded it. And there is no Big Clock in the Sky to tell us which one is really right. The only thing that is the same for all observers is an "interval" that is a combination of space-distance and time-distance (zero if the event happened a second ago 186,000 miles away, the speed of light.) This is an unavoidable consequence of the fact that light, the bearer of information, does not move at an infinite speed. Compared to distances in the cosmos, which has been expanding at the speed of light for 10 or 15 billion years, light's speed of some 186,000 miles a second is slow. Many such consequences of relativity seemed to defy common sense. But common sense, as Einstein observed, is only yesterday's science, which was itself once astonishing. By now we have probably gotten used to the Einsteinian world though it remains far less accessible than the Newtonian one. At first it was passing strange and became the subject of jokes, the burden of which was that no one could understand it. (So too the psychoanalyst, the "shrink," the strange little man behind the couch, was matter for amusement; Einstein shared with Freud, himself a keen analyst of humor, this tendency to become the target of popular laughter. This was rather more good-humored than the gibes at modern art.[3])

The most startling of the paradoxes of relativity was time dilation, or the lengthening of time, for an observer at rest, of a body in rapid motion. If you should make a rapid trip around the cosmos, travelling at somewhere near the speed of light, and return a year later (by your perfectly accurate calendar), you would find upon returning home that your friends all thought, say, two years had elapsed. If you had made a date to meet someone after a year, you would be hopelessly late, through no fault of your own, and she would probably have married someone else long since. It is also true, according to Einstein's theory, that the faster you go the heavier and squatter you get. This increased mass comes from increased energy; energy has mass, and vice versa. The famous $E = mc^2$ formula (c being the speed of light) emerged from this brilliant spate of theorizing by the young Einstein. No wonder it has been claimed that no other human mind was capable of this feat (though this is questionable if we mean that no one would have ever thought of it). Though Poincaré and Minkowski among others were fumbling towards the truths of relativity, Einstein alone summed them up succinctly and masterfully. "Most of the other great results of Einstein might have been produced within a few years by someone else," Otto Frisch stated, "but I think in this case nothing but the extraordinary power and concentration of Einstein would have been enough." Others, however, including Einstein himself, have thought his general relativity theory even more original. Someone else, he thought, sooner or later would have come up with the special relativity theory. And indeed historians of science painstakingly reconstructing this path of discovery tend to view it as a collective achievement. So it was too with other great scientific discoveries and inventions: Darwin had his Wallace, Freud his Janet, i.e., people who almost got to the same place at the same time.[4]

Einstein began working on the general theory of relativity, though between 1905 and 1911 he was also deeply interested in deciding whether light was photon particles as he had argued in 1905, or a wave as in some contexts it seemed to be. He concentrated on his revision of Newton's hallowed law of gravitation between 1911 and 1916. "No advance whatever had been made in explaining gravitation during the 230 years since Newton, although the action at a distance that it seems to demand had always been repugnant," Bertrand Russell remarked. Most scientists considered this a case of fixing what wasn't broken, since the elegantly simple Newtonian inverse square law succeeded splendidly, there being only a few obscure cases which it failed to explain. It is true that the assumption of absolute space and time might be queried on philosophical grounds, and that "action at a distance," the "force" of gravity, was in itself mysterious. One knew only its formula, and that was enough: rather like a medicine that worked, though no one knew how or why.

Einstein was to show that his idea worked better. Elimination of space and time as independent qualities, along with the "ether" of space, forced reconsideration of Newtonian gravity. How could there be instantaneous action at a distance if time is not the same all over the universe, and if there is no medium to transmit this impulse? Einstein held that the force of gravity is not an "attraction," action at a distance, but the way in which a body moves through the curved geodesics of space-time, choosing the easiest route. By a crude analogy (the situation is really not capable of being portrayed visually as the world has ceased to be common-sensical), space-time is filled with hills and valleys. Planets circle the sun because it is easier to go around a mountain than climb straight up it. Objects determine the properties of the space-time field around them, causing distortion of it by their presence, like electromagnetic "fields." A magnet does not attract a piece of iron by some mysterious "force" but because it engenders a certain physical condition in its vicinity. Like a fish swimming in the water, a star distorts the geometry of the space-time through which it moves. Space becomes curved in the presence of matter. Gravitation is a part of the geometry of space-time (a curved geometry, remember). Einstein declared that "gravity is due to a change in the curvature of space-time, produced by the presence of matter."

A great excitement seized the public mind when a rare total eclipse of the sun on May 30, 1919, provided the opportunity to test Einstein's theory. The distinguished British scientist Arthur Eddington directed worldwide observations. The Treaty of Versailles was about to be signed at that same moment, but it was quite secondary in importance to the Einstein-Newton match. Einstein was judged to have won. SPACE CAUGHT BENDING, newspaper headlines ran with only normal journalistic inaccuracy. The Einstein theory predicted that light from a distant star would curve as it entered the gravitational field of the sun, light being in effect a form of matter. This phenomenon was allegedly observed on that famous day, though the measurement was so infinitesimally small that a little doubt has always remained. Einstein's general relativity account of gravity has received support from other quarters: explaining, as Newtonianism could not, the observed slight precession or wobble in the orbits of the planets, and the gravitational red shift, i.e., the lower frequency of light emitted in a region of strong gravitational attraction as seen by a distant observer. Later, "black holes" offered another sensational proof.[5] The general relativity theory, too, has been called "the most original conception that the mind of man ever created."

If nuclear power was the eventual upshot of $E = mc^2$, laser beams ultimately derive from Einstein's conception of light as a form of radiation which emits energy in quantum bursts. But Einstein created more drama in the 1920s when he broke with the majority of scientists on the question of "quantum mechanics," the behavior of electrons inside atoms. Having initially argued that light and other forms of radiation are particles, Einstein had second thoughts. What chiefly disturbed him was the emergence of uncertainty, of riddles that seemed unresolvable or defied traditional scientific canons of absolute clarity and predictability. The work on quantum mechanics that went forward in the 1920s under the aegis of a brilliant crew of youngsters, all in some sense Einstein's children, was to eventuate in the Uncertainty Principle, abhorrent to Einstein's sense of cosmic order. (According to his famous motto, God may be subtle but he is not wicked, for he would not deceive us.)

By 1927, after all, Einstein was nearly fifty and had led the advance guard for twenty years. Others like Niels Bohr, the Copenhagen wizard, had studied under Planck and Thomson and Rutherford. A whole generation of younger men and women at home in the strange new world of Planck and Einstein was rising. Youth seemed to be especially suited to theoretical physics with its heavy mathematical component. Einstein had had his moment of supreme inspiration when about twenty-five. Now people like De Broglie, Dirac, Heisenberg, Schrödinger, and Pauli were becoming equally as creative in their twenties. The problem that absorbed them, and to which Einstein now returned, was one of epochal, dramatic significance. It seemed to involve the very foundations of science as it had always been understood.

The strangeness of the subatomic world appeared in a number of ways. The electrons within the atom—evidently the smallest units of matter[6]—behaved at times as waves and at other times as particles, something inconceivable. Scientists spoke of "wavicles" and "wave mechanics." Two electrons could be in the same place at once. Even more disturbingly, it was impossible to know both their position and their velocity. Nobody before quantum theory, as Bertrand Russell observed, ever doubted that at any given moment a physical body is at some definite place and moving with some definite speed. But the more accurately you determined the place of a particle, the less accurately could you measure its velocity, and vice versa. In fact, we know only certain equations of which the interpretation was obscure. These apply to statistical probabilities for large numbers of electrons over periods of time; the individual ones elude exact prediction. An anarchic universe, Russell suggested, filled with a nonconformist minority. For example, quantum mechanics can calculate the proportion of a radioactive material which will decay over a stated period of time—10 percent in the next thousand years, say—but how long it will be before the next alpha particle is extruded or which one it will be defies prediction. Like the paradoxes of relativity, this is not just a deficiency in our research which might in the future be overcome; it is an absolute limit set by the nature of things. One reason for this is that we reach the limits of observation because we must use particles (gamma rays) to observe other particles, and in so doing we interfere with them. The scientist cannot stand outside what he is observing, he is a part of it. Interesting, and perhaps encouraging to the poor humanist or social scientist, but alarming to the whole scientific tradition; man reaches a frontier he cannot cross and must give up the quest for certainty.

Bohr had visualized a miniature solar system within the atom, the electrons circling the nucleus-sun, except that these little planets for some reason jumped and switched orbits instantaneously, obviously behaving wholly unlike the solar systems we know. Broglie and Schrödinger visualized a kind of chamber filled with peculiar wave movements—waves of what? Of probability, was one mystifying answer. Some thought it a mistake to attempt to visualize a physical model comparable to everyday human experience; the world is best thought of as a set of mathematical equations. If we free ourselves from such earthbound prejudices, we can imagine all sorts of things—a *fifth* dimension, or a dozen of them.

Attempts to conceptualize this impasse took several forms. Perhaps the world itself is unclear and fuzzy. Bohr speculated that it might be complementary, i.e., ambivalent, each thing having also its opposite. Or perhaps the external world is clear; it is our human minds that are flawed, unable because of some inherent limitation to get the world in focus. Perhaps a better language or new mathematical tools might clear matters up. To mathematicize the world, however, risks not only making it incomprehensible to the vast innumerate majority, but also mystifying it in a way that destroys the very premises of modern science. And our mental limitations may be built into our mathematics, which is after all only a form of language. (Mathematics itself experienced doubts about its status; the path from Hilbert, 1900, to Gödel, 1931, in mathematical philosophy was comparable to that from Planck and Einstein to Bohr and Heisenberg in physics, one of increasing doubts about objectivity and consistency.)

Einstein resisted the drift to uncertainty and indeterminacy. He did not like wavicles and probabilities because they offended his sense of cosmic order, in which was embedded his deep esthetic sense. Theories must be elegant, not ungainly. This included simplicity and clarity, those classical virtues. (Einstein the musician loved Mozart.) There must be an underlying order remaining to be discovered—"hidden variables." If you see me lurching about wildly and leap to the conclusion that I am mad or drunk, this may be because concealed from your sight is a slippery surface that I am trying to walk on. Quantum theory must be incomplete. There is something more not yet visible that will explain its apparent absurdities. Refusing to accept the finality of indeterminacy, Einstein used his famous imagination to devise thought experiments embarrassing to supporters of quantum mechanics. This was a matter of Einstein's faith in a God who would not so cruelly deceive us. One suspects it was also a matter of the man's stubborn perversity; he would never run with the crowd, even if it was in a race he had started. The encounter in 1927 with Bohr and Heisenberg at the Solvay conference was memorable, but Einstein was judged to have lost.[7] These limitations of knowledge have to be accepted. Practically speaking, it does not make much difference. There may be one chance in a billion billion that an electron will defy the rules. Statistical averages, if exact, are good enough: if you know that next year the batting average of the New York Yankees as a team will be .299, you may not need to know the average of each individual player. There is knowledge enough without asking for everything.

There was no bitterness in this debate; it was all a glorious game, which these jugglers with cosmic immensities carried on more lightheartedly than the solemn psychiatrists of Freud's circle. Unlike Freud and Jung, Einstein and Bohr remained close friends. Caught smiling once and asked what it was about, Einstein answered that he was thinking of the galaxies. Absurd, indeed, to think that there are billions of them each made up of billions of stars like our own sun, so that we become one speck of sand on a beach as big as the whole Caribbean. In 1930 in California, Einstein looked through the Mt. Wilson telescope where Hubble, glimpsing stars 800,000 light years away, showed that galaxies are moving away from us at a speed proportionate to their distance. But no more absurd than that are particles that occupy no space at all and live less than a billionth of a second. Physicists later began to revel in the absurdity, choosing a word from James Joyce's fantastic novel *Finnegans Wake* to bestow on a sub-particle the name "quark" (with varieties named "strange" and "magic"). "A tolerance for crazy hypotheses" is one of the things modern science should teach us, Martin Gardner says. The Bohr circle at Copenhagen by propounding the Uncertainty Principle made it into an axiom. But in many quarters there was a good deal of dismayed concern at science's abandonment one by one of its treasured exactitudes and certainties.

How far Einstein diverged from the mainstream is seen in his next and perhaps last great project, unified field theory. Not many other scientists were interested in it. In his later years at Princeton, before his death in 1955, Einstein was regarded as rather passé. There has been some more recent revival of interest in his unified field theory, which described physical reality not as particles but as areas of influence, rather like knots in a string. The particles had betrayed him; he wanted to do away with them altogether. Yet scientific attention focused on those particles in the ensuing decades. If they do not exist, spending billions of dollars on tunnels fifteen or fifty miles long in which to smash them is a strange waste. Up to 200 of them named leptons, mesons, gluons, neutrinos, quarks, etc. were identified. The two forces that Einstein struggled to bring under one theoretical roof, electromagnetism and general relativity (gravity, motion) increased to four with the addition of the Weak Force that holds particles together and the Strong Force binding the atoms and molecules.

It was the latter force, we know, that proved the most spectacular of all consequences of the new physics, the atomic bomb. The formula $E = mc^2$ went back to Einstein, of course. Einstein's friend Otto Hahn discovered that the uranium atom could be split; he joined forces on this with the remarkable Austrian Jewess Lise Meitner in 1938 (who fled from the Nazis at the same time as Freud, coming to the United States). James Chadwick, Rutherford's student, had discovered the neutron at Cavendish in 1932—a bullet eventually used to bombard the atom's nucleus, something performed by Enrico Fermi in Rome in 1934. The roots of this revolution go back to the Curies' discovery that atoms can decay, and to Rutherford's achievement in 1919, at the same time as the corroboration of Einstein's general relativity theory, when he showed that atoms can in fact be transmuted. In this groundwork toward development of the bomb Einstein played no direct part. His famous letter to President Franklin Roosevelt in August 1939, pointing out the need to develop an atomic bomb before the Nazis did, was written chiefly at the instigation of Fermi.

Einstein himself had settled in the United States after 1933, when, out of the country when Hitler came to power, he renounced his German citizenship and refused to return to his homeland. The Nazi regime proclaimed him a degenerate modernist and pro-Bolshevik traitor and used him as a symbolic scapegoat for its rebellion against the whole modern world, for he was Jewish, internationalist, and revolutionary. Einstein had not previously been anti-German, certainly not during the years of the Weimar Republic in the 1920s. He was intermittently a militant pacifist and had praised Lenin but was critical of the Soviet Union, at least privately. He joined the Zionist movement in 1921, converted by Chaim Weizmann. He called himself a socialist, because a "planned economy" appealed to his sense of order, yet worried about the excessive powers this might bring to the bureaucrats.[8] There was a certain childlike innocence about Einstein's politics, as there was about his whole personality. The subtlety of his scientific thought stands in stark contrast to his political ideas, except that the quest for simple clarity marked both. The argument that in politics an intellectual rationalism is usually wrong and occasionally disastrous may find support in such examples as Einstein and Bertrand Russell. Be that as it may, along with many others Einstein had renounced his pacifism by 1935 as the need for resisting the Nazi menace grew evident.

"If, indeed, the sub-atomic energy in the stars is being freely used to maintain their great furnaces," Eddington had remarked many years before, "it seems to bring a little nearer to fulfillment our dream of controlling this latent power for the well-being of the human race—or for its suicide." Nearly three quarters of a century later the question remains open. Nuclear energy is widely used as a source of energy, contaminating less dangerously than the coal burning which threatens us with an excess of CO^2, but it is also assailed by many whose view of it as evil is almost a religious obsession. Nuclear weapons in one perspective have prevented major war for a generation and will continue to do so; in another, they will sooner or later destroy life on earth. Einstein, of course, cannot be held responsible for nuclear power any more than hundreds of other scientists, technologists, and politicians. We can attribute the development of laser beams more directly to his insight that light is a form of radiant energy.

If we raise the issue of estimating Einstein's influence, we come across problems similar to those encountered with Freud: for one thing, how do we separate this one person from the much larger movement of which he was indeed the node but not at all the whole? And how do we distinguish him from a general zeitgeist that was even larger than the movement? Shy, cerebral, almost exclusively absorbed in his scientific work, Einstein fits even less well than Freud into the "flaming youth" spirit of revolt that tried to appropriate him as its symbol. Yet we know there *was* something of the rebel, something of the jeering outsider in his personality as well as in his appearance. To others he was the pure intellect, the epitome of Man Thinking, his luminous eyes and waving mane radiating this hopeful vision of mind struggling to understand the deepest, most complex secrets of nature. (The picture of the young Einstein revealed in the recently discovered early letters to his wife, to be sure, is of a far earthier creature.)

When the age of Einstein supplanted that of Newton, something of comprehensibility was lost. "God said, Let Newton be, and all was light"—to Pope's famous epigram Belloc riposted, "The Devil, crying ho!/Let Einstein be, restored the status quo." In a news story of March 8, 1987, the director of the Boston Science Museum deplored widespread scientific illiteracy and declining interest in science, noting that "children lose their interest in science by the time they're in the eighth grade." Millions of people attend museums to gape at projections of astronauts walking on the moon, or robots that can play tic-tac-toe, but less than 10 percent can state the difference between astronomy and astrology; much evidence suggests a larger percentage follow the latter than the former. If, as a 1983 study by John Miller of Northern Illinois University found, 93 percent of adults are scientifically illiterate, the reason surely is not far to seek. C. T. R. Wilson, a noted British scientist of Einstein's generation and deviser of the cloud chamber, thought in his youth that the principles of physics ought to be comprehensible to even the simplest laborer (every barmaid, he said). Now the most advanced scientists disagree about them in works of impenetrable difficulty. No one without command of advanced mathematics need even bother trying. Physics and astronomy have become the realm of the bizarre, exciting for a few adepts but utterly beyond the reach of the vast majority. It is doubtful if any vision of the universe communicates to them, as it once did to everyone, a steadying image of serenity, security, immutability, and divine governance.

A host of intellects tried to explain the new physical universe to the public at large—people as distinguished as Bertrand Russell, James Jeans, Einstein's friend Max Born, Einstein himself, Max Planck too. They usually concluded with statements about the "mysterious universe," the impossibility of visualizing it, the limits of science, its ever-changing nature, the loss of certitude, the gap between reality and scientific knowledge: "the world as science sees it is not the world as it really is" (Joseph Needham). Planck, who wrote much about the philosophical implications of the new science in his later years, was almost as dismayed as Einstein at what he had done. "'Tis only one great thought the less," sighed the old Thomas Hardy, surveying the wreckage of human pretentiousness from Copernicus through Darwin to Einstein in his "Drinking Song":

> And now comes Einstein with a notion
> Not yet quite clear
> To many here—
> That there's no time, no space, no motion. . .

We "weep for the lost ages," Auden wrote, "before Because became As If, or rigid certainty/ The Chances Are . . ."

But when one got rid of the layer of prejudices deposited by the old science, the new one grew more supportable, with advantages as well as disadvantages. Some found the unpredictable, paradoxical quality of this modernist world-picture exciting. "I like relativity and quantum theories," D. H. Lawrence declared, "because I don't understand them, and they make me feel as if space shifted . . . and as if the atom were an impulsive thing, always changing its mind" (*Complete Poems*). Modernism in the arts, growing up along side the new science, made some use of it. "Space and time died yesterday!" the Futurist manifesto of 1909 exulted. Einstein's findings encouraged the feeling that new rules can be made, anything is possible. A cubist painting or a twelve-tone, serialist musical composition broke with tradition as sharply and in somewhat the same way as relativity and quantum theory. The artistic modernists wanted to escape the "real" world of everyday objects to perceive deeper relations, abstract structures. Yet, as Linda Dalrymple Henderson has pointed out[9], the first Cubists did not cite or evidently know about Einstein, though they did know Poincaré. The artistic evolution that produced Cubism stemmed chiefly from the earlier Impressionist painters. More monographs such as hers are needed to explore the complex relationships between art, science, and the general zeitgeist that contained them both. Like Freud, Einstein had little sympathy for modern art, though the painter Paul Klee was a close friend. But the gestation period for modernism in all branches of the arts (c. 1905– 1913) corresponds so closely to Einstein's emergence that some influences were inevitable. The pioneer Swiss architect Le Corbusier, for example, spent the years from 1907 to 1911 absorbing "modern ideas" in visits to Vienna, Paris, and Berlin, as well as revisiting the classics in Italy and Greece. The architect Mendelsohn designed an Einstein Tower in the 1920s.

Nineteenth-century science, positivist and materialistic, had tended to claim a monopoly of true knowledge, dismissing art and especially religion as relics of barbarism. The new science deflated such imperialistic claims, leaving a place for art as well as religion, even mysticism. Einstein himself acknowledged an influence from Dostoyevsky; the great scientist Wolfgang Pauli from Carl Jung. (Jung and Pauli tried to collaborate on a study of parapsychology. Pauli's famous "exclusion principle" was indeed as strange a magic as anything claimed by the occult.) Science, Pauli knew, had departed in the time of Kepler from mysticism; now it seemed to be returning to it. The German physicist von Weizsaecker studied Indian religion in search of scientific insights. A historian of witchcraft, Charles Hoyt, suggests that contemporary physics is not irrelevant to his subject! The rigid boundaries between art, religion, and science tended to dissolve, and one finds numerous cases of physicists who have strong secondary esthetic interests. One of the leading *Finnegans Wake* interpreters, for example, is a scientist whose avocation is Joyce studies.

It is interesting if speculative to relate scientific relativity to other forms of relativism or multiperspectivism that have so notably marked modern literature and thought. Walter Pater, writing in 1866, had already discerned as the leading tendency in "modern" thought "its cultivation of the 'relative' spirit in place of the 'absolute.'" Between 1902 and 1904, at almost exactly the same time as Einstein's early work, Henry James published the last three novels he would ever complete. In these books, the dean of Anglo-American novelists launched a new course which seems almost as revolutionary as the new science, and somewhat similar. Most nineteenth-century novels assumed an absolute truth, unveiled by the "omniscient" author. James' last novels along with some others of this era (e.g. André Gide in France) undermine this authorial omniscience. We do not feel sure that we fully know the characters in the novel; indeed, we are led to feel, a bit uncomfortably, that they cannot be known; they have no essence, truth depends on the point of view. Modern literature is filled with such ambiguous meanings, new and subversive narrative strategies, characters in search of an author rather than vice versa. And the same is true of genres such as history and anthropology. The old certainty that scholars can by careful research find *the* truth about the past began to be corroded by doubts about the possibility of objectivity, by awareness that there is no one past but as many as there are historians, who must partly manufacture the truth about past events out of their own time and place-conditioned consciousness. Albert Einstein's own religion was a kind of old-fashioned deism. Like Freud (and Marx), he lost his orthodox Jewish faith early, replacing it with a scientist's belief in a rational order of things. God does not play deceitful games with us, though he tests us with difficult riddles. (*Raffiniert* is Herr Gott but not *boshaft*, in Einstein's native tongue.) That is why Einstein could not accept quantum mechanics; as soon as he saw it leading to indeterminacy, uncertainty principles, strange paradoxes, he shied off from it, murmuring (in effect) if I had known it was going to come to this I would never have started it. (I could have thought of something like that, he said of quantum atomic theory, but it would mean the end of physics so I didn't!)

If twentieth-century science has fallen into obscurity and even perversity, and if Einstein is the leader of this science, his image is, oddly, a totally different thing. The image is one of stupendous brainpower harnessed to loveable, childlike simplicity; amiable eccentricity, perhaps, with humor, a twinkling eye, and a love of common humanity. In his later years a familiar and revered world figure, today as widely known as any individual of the twentieth century, Einstein avoided most of the political-ideological rancor that tarnished the names of intellectual giants such as Heidegger, Russell, and Sartre, and the controversy that for different reasons surrounds Freud and Joyce. He seemed an open-minded friend of truth, seeking it with absolute integrity. During World War I, when practically everyone surrendered to the spirit of nationalism, Einstein remained one of a few relatively uncorrupted intellectuals. He became a symbol of defiance of Nazi intolerance and likewise of Stalinism, despite the fact that the American FBI suspected him of pro-Communist attitudes.

Both the Nazis and the Communists, who condemned Einstein, argued that science is not objective but serves the social order of which it is a part. Hence there is no absolute truth; it is national, or class, truth. Some of Einstein's German colleagues (e.g. Johannes Stark, a Nobel Prize winner and a pioneer in quantum theory) adopted Hitler's line and proclaimed the need for science to be National Socialist. These men erred. Truth may be elusive, in the end unattainable; but the quest for it must be untrammeled, fearless, free. In the end this is what Albert Einstein stands for most of all.

Notes

[1] A panel at the Amerian Association for Advancement of Science meeting in New Orleans, February 1990, debated the issue, raised by feminists, of Einstein's scientific debt to his first wife. There is little real evidence that Mileva Maric made vital contributions to relativity theory, but it is certain that she was a competent scientist who after 1914 was stuck with the children and received little help from Albert.

[2] One of Einstein's three historic papers of 1905 dealt with the erratic behavior of molecules, a riddle Clerk Maxwell had worked on.

[3] A limerick of the '20s embraced all of them:
> Of the notable family named Stein
> There is Gert, there is Ep and there's Ein.
> Gert's prose is the bunk, Ep's sculpture is junk,
> And no one can understand Ein.

[4] W. L. Fadner, "Did Einstein Really Discover 'E = mc²'?" *American Journal of Physics*, vol. 56 (1988), 114–22, finds Einstein's claim justified though it has been disputed and "several people participated" in the development of the formula relating mass to energy. Frederick Soddy, a name few have probably heard of, produced almost the same equation as Einstein's in 1904.

[5] Special relativity has also been confirmed in various ways, for example, by the observed fact that the unstable subatomic particles called muons, which come from outer space, are more abundant at lower levels of altitude; the only explanation is that their life is prolonged through time dilation—time is stretched out in rapid motion, particles live longer when going faster.

[6] At this time, i.e. the 1920s, it was thought that the electrons or negatively charged particles that circle the positively charged nucleus were all alike. Discovery of neutrons and then scores of other particles differing in mass, charge, length of life, movement, etc. lay ahead. Many of these emerged from bombardment of atomic nuclei in the 1950s, disclosing a strange miscellany of particles buried there. The "proton" proved to be divisible into lesser particles.

[7] This verdict still holds. For an account of recent experiments that seemed to answer an Einstein objection and support quantum theory, see P. C. W. Davies and J. R. Brown, eds. *The Ghost in the Atom: A Discussion of the Mysteries of Quantum Physics* (1986).

[8] See his "Why Socialism?" (1949), in *Out of My Later Years* (1950).

[9] *The Fourth Dimension and Non-Euclidean Geometry in Modern Art* (1983).

WITTGENSTEIN

I<small>F</small> all our five figures were geniuses, the one who came closest to the popular image of a "mad genius" was probably Ludwig Wittgenstein. A little of this aura surrounds Einstein, of course, but it is mixed with one of benevolent simplicity. *Finnegans Wake* has impressed more than a few as a crazy book, but Joyce himself was seemingly a most ordinary personality. It was another story with Wittgenstein. Most of his friends and acquaintances, who usually agreed that he was a genius, thought him touched with a kind of divine insanity. Wittgenstein himself in an argument with Bertrand Russell, when reproached with departing from accepted norms, once declared roundly "God save me from sanity." Russell added with his dry wit "God certainly will."

Wittgenstein comes close, in Carl Jung's classification of personality types, to the introverted intuitionist, a type that produces religious prophets. They dredge up images from their interior consciousness and project these onto the world, convinced of their urgent importance. The difference is that this man was a saint of rationalism, not of faith. He certainly felt that he had a mission and suffered deeply from not being able to fulfill it: "He is morbidly afraid he may die before he has put the Theory of Types to rights," his friend David Pinsent observed in 1913. "I ought to have done something positive with my life, to have become a star in the sky; instead of which I remained stuck on earth," young Wittgenstein said. He felt he had a great truth to deliver and suffered torment to the verge of suicide when he thought he was not delivering it. He had an extreme kind of what Freud called super-ego, a conscience or sense of guilt at not serving the human community faithfully enough. Such a trait is presumably implanted by a powerful father figure; and this was present in the great Wittgenstein family. Three of Ludwig's siblings were suicides, while his brother Paul became famous for making himself a successful concert pianist despite the loss of an arm in the war (for him Maurice Ravel wrote the compelling "Concerto for Left Hand"). This most unusual family, drawn from the cultivated *haute bourgeoisie* of Vienna, had produced engineers, industrialists, scientists, and artists. Originally Jewish, but assimilated into Austro-German culture, it was imbued with an intense ethic of achievement.

Though he eventually gave away most of his money, Ludwig Wittgenstein always had enough to make livelihood no problem, especially for a person of his simple wants; he had a natural and total scorn for material things beyond the barest creature comforts. Perhaps only the scion of an extremely rich family (Ludwig's father has been called the Andrew Carnegie of Austria) could develop such an attitude. Beyond this, he had of course the kind of mental equipment that marks genius. The combination produced an absolute commitment to pure thought, along with a scorn for any compromises, that the average person would classify as fanaticism. The young Wittgenstein once agonized because he had given in to Russell's invitation to watch the Oxford-Cambridge boat race and thus wasted an afternoon. ("He explained that the way we had spent the afternoon was so vile that we ought not to live," Russell related.)

He would appear at Russell's rooms at 4 A.M. and talk logic for four hours without a halt. He was, in this respect, quite often a crashing bore, a person with no small talk, no ordinary human interests. Though he much needed an audience of one intellectual equal, Wittgenstein was antisocial to a degree none of our other geniuses approached. They all in their various ways were gregarious beings, with an immense circle of friends and many social activities—even Einstein by comparison to Wittgenstein was a social butterfly. Wittgenstein never married or came close to it (he is the only one of our group suspected of homosexuality); he had little interest in his own family and not many close friends. He was the only one who could have lived by choice, as he was wont to do, in a remote Norwegian fishing village. Likewise, only Wittgenstein would seriously have considered becoming a monk. Once he tried to become a village school teacher in Austria. Freud, Joyce, and Sartre are inseparable from urban life; Einstein from the scientific community. Wittgenstein fled from all such busy haunts of men, ending his days among Irish villagers. When he taught at Oxford he never wanted to visit London (except when there was a convention of philosophers), preferring to take nature walks. Frequently he fled to Norway. He published very little—one short book and one article. With his small number of seminar students he simply thought out loud—an awesome performance to students, who said they had never seen anyone thinking. Yet like Nietzsche's Zarathustra, Wittgenstein had an abhorrence of followers. It is true that he mellowed with age. Though often he had been fiercely unhappy, he said on his death bed he had had "a wonderful life." We believe him; he had spent all of it pursuing Truth.

Wittgenstein's personality cries out for psychoanalysis. His inflexibility and perfectionism, inexorably high standards, and extreme demands on himself went along with stormy relations with friends, on whom he also made large demands. Narcissist and obsessive, Wittgenstein fought with himself as well as with others a good part of his life. He was a driven and tormented figure, this greatest of twentieth-century philosophers. That is why he had such charisma, why he seemed to many hardly less than divine (Jesus had had such qualities), why he has become like Einstein a cult figure.

The demon that seized hold of Wittgenstein in his earlier years was the demon of Logic. He came to England from Vienna initially to continue an engineering education which he had begun at the technical college of Charlottenburg in Berlin. There are some parallels with Einstein. Ludwig had scientific interests and was said to have considered studying physics until deterred by the suicide in 1906 of Ludwig Boltzmann, a Vienna professor whom he much admired (but who was a foe of relativity). Wittgenstein disliked Mach because of the latter's style; there was a deep esthetic element in Wittgenstein which suggests he was a kind of cross between Einstein and Joyce—except that Wittgenstein, no more than Einstein, or Freud, cared much for *modern* art. Refusing to listen to Richard Strauss's *Salome*, he said he belonged to a world that vanished with the death of Schumann. Wittgenstein had Romantic tastes, contrasting with Einstein's eighteenth-century classicism.

Wittgenstein's interest in aeronautics led the handsome, slight-of-build nineteen-year-old to Manchester in 1908. Mechanically skillful, the young Austrian took part in important work on airplane engines (including the first jet engines) in this pioneer era of aviation. According to some accounts he was imaginative but a little too volatile and impatient for experimental engineering science. Like the Wright Brothers, he conceived the romantic ambition of designing and flying his own airplane, but evidently never did so.

Rutherford, among other eminent scientists and mathematicians, was at Manchester at this time. Serious scientific and philosophical interests were never far from Wittgenstein's mind. Bertrand Russell told the story of how the young would-be aviator came to him one day in 1911 at Cambridge and said "Tell me if I am a complete idiot or not. If I am, I will become an aeronautical engineer. [!] If not, I shall become a philosopher." Russell asked him to write something over the holiday and after reading the first line told him "You must not become an engineer." Like many of Russell's stories this one is a little too pat to be true, yet in essence something like this did happen. A passionate curiosity about what underlies mathematics had gripped Wittgenstein, and Russell—co-author in 1910 with Alfred North Whitehead of the epochal *Principia Mathematica*—was probably the world's leading authority on the philosophy of mathematics. His only rival was the older Viennese sage Gottfried Frege, who apparently advised Wittgenstein to seek out Russell.

Wittgenstein became involved with the problems of Frege's and Russell's attempts to express mathematical principles in logical form. Russell's paper "On Denoting," written in 1905, was part of his intense early preoccupation with making language more exact and logical. In seeking like Frege to establish arithmetic on secure logical foundations, Russell tried to demonstrate that the purely logical notions of identity, class, class-membership, and class-equivalence suffice for constructing the series of natural numbers. His "theory of types" was designed to overcome obstacles in the way of this goal, notably the paradox of "the class of classes that are not members of themselves."

All this in Wittgenstein's mind raised questions about the status of such logical propositions; do they exist objectively, a language of nature ("the laws of truth itself," as Frege held) or are they thoughts in human minds which bear no direct relationship to the external world? Such questions were so rarefied that only a few people in the world understood them. When G. E. Moore's wife heard Moore, Russell, and Wittgenstein engaged in an excited discussion about whether there are three things in the world or only two, she was understandably as mystified as anyone else would have been. Russell claimed that Wittgenstein once stubbornly denied that it could be proven that no rhinoceros (or in another version hippopotamus) was in Russell's room. We may be sure that some logical point of substance was in Ludwig's mind.

It is clear at any rate that, as Ludwig wrote in his notebook in 1916, "my work has broadened out from the foundations of logic to the nature of the world." Well it might. As we know from our encounter with Einstein, the new scientific revolution raised very sharply the question of how words—like atom, electron, force, matter—are related to the real world. Obviously they are not the *same* as the things they try to describe. Nor are they a "direct copy" of it. We experience sense data: colors on a photographic plate, for instance. The words we employ to transcribe this data into language belong to another order, which tries to correspond with the real world as best it can but sometimes barely succeeds in this, perhaps even becoming an obstacle. "Atoms are not things, electrons are no longer things in the sense of classical physics. . . . When we get down to the atomic level, the objective world in space and time no longer exists, and the mathematical symbols of theoretical analysis refer merely to possibilities not to facts." So remarked Werner Heisenberg a few years later. The hard, precise, "real" physical world seemed to dissolve into "nothing more than a shadow of our imagination" (Mara Beller).

The question of mathematics' status as a special kind of language had been raised before. Clerk Maxwell had produced a set of equations leading to the discovery of various rays which these equations predicted. This mathematization of physics continued, to the dismay of some older laboratory scientists. It was not a question of finding experimental truths and then giving these a mathematical expression; it was a question, it seemed, of deducing the nature of reality from equations found by mathematical reason. Or even of dispensing with sense experience altogether, concocting a purely mathematical construction of the atom with no pretense of relating to anything material. Is the world a set of equations? Or do we perhaps impose these equations arbitrarily on the world just as we impose words? Such questions had arisen in the last years of the nineteenth century; Maxwell, Mach, Poincaré, Bradley were wrestling with them. "The frank realization that physical science is concerned with a world of shadows," was an idea that Arthur Eddington, in his widely read *The Nature of the Physical World*, called the most significant of modern "advances." Such bewildering perspectives raised the keenest issues of logic and ontology, while at the same time, to the dismay of many old-fashioned scientists, they trespassed on mysticism.

Wittgenstein's life and thought exhibited a radical ambivalence or dualism between the analytical and the poetical, the rational and the religious, which psychoanalysts would no doubt find significant, but which also reflected the scientific-philosophical crisis of his time. He was at most times the severely professional, highly technical logician. The sharp tool of his intellect deconstructed all systems. It was he who declared (*Tractatus*, 4.003) that "most of the propositions and questions to be found in philosophical works are not false but nonsensical." In common with others of the school he was long thought to represent, the Logical Positivists, Wittgenstein held that philosophy ought not to build theories or systems, or even, as such, search for Truth; its purpose is strictly a logical one, to clarify those confusions into which people fall when they attempt to think. It is "a struggle against the bewitchment of our intelligence by language." Philosophy finds no knowledge of its own, there are no metaphysical truths; finding knowledge (true propositions) is the province of the sciences. "Philosophy gives no picture of reality and can neither confirm nor confute scientific investigations."

Upon careful analysis any other kind of knowledge than that of scientific investigation turns out to be nonsense. "The reason why philosophical problems are posed at all is owing to a misunderstanding of language." The function of philosophy is thus a dual one: to show the futility of all that has previously passed for philosophizing (attempts by verbal trickery to answer unanswerable questions); and to help the natural and human sciences methodologically, by demystifying and clarifying their terminology.

Subsequently Wittgenstein was to find another use for philosophy, rather akin to Freud's: to solve some of our life problems by showing us their roots in linguistic confusion. He passed from stringent logical analysis to an ethical, almost mystical dimension in the course of writing the one book he published in his lifetime, the *Tractatus Logico-Philosophicus*, as it was titled when translated into English. (Logical-philosophical treatise; in German, *Logisch-philosophische Abhandlung*). Published in 1922, at about the same time as Joyce's *Ulysses* and T. S. Eliot's *The Waste Land*, the *Tractatus* became a manifesto of modernism, a cult book, as obscure and exciting as those literary masterpieces redolent of postwar intellectual and moral crisis.

During the Great War of 1914–1918 Wittgenstein like many European intellectuals found the experience fascinating as well as terrifying; he tested himself against every hardship, fought with great bravery in the Austrian army, and was decorated several times. He could of course—the odds were in its favor—have been killed along with so many million others. That he survived was not because he avoided danger. Early in the war he found, quite by accident, Tolstoy's exposition of the Christian Gospels with its message that "for a man living not the personal but the common life of the spirit, there is no death."[1] He carried the book with him throughout the war. The dismaying end of the fighting in 1918 left him seared and confused.

Begun in his often acerbic debates with Russell and Moore, labored on in solitude in a Norwegian hut in 1914, carried around with him on the battlefield during the war, the *Tractatus* had as romantic a provenance as one could want. Wittgenstein had considerable difficulty finding a publisher for it. It was turned down by Cambridge! Printed defectively in an obscure German scientific journal in 1921, it was translated into English and published by Kegan Paul, Trench, Trubner & Co., with the aid of Russell and F. P. Ramsey, in 1922. The title, reminiscent of Spinoza, was suggested by G. E. Moore.[2] The *Tractatus* was trenchant, compressed, gnomic; its 20,000 words could be read in an afternoon but puzzled over for years. Jean-Paul Sartre once spoke of "the ambiguous delight of understanding without understanding—the destiny of the world." This could certainly be applied to the many who have read the *Tractatus*. It had a kind of esthetic elegance (it has been set to music) at which in fact its author deliberately aimed: a piece of prose poetry disguised as an exercise in the deepest sort of logical thought, or vice versa. Spare, laconic, cryptic, it was like a Kandinsky painting or a Le Corbusier building. It was hauntingly eloquent, as well as forbiddingly profound. Its propositions, numbered and subnumbered, were as bracing as the Norwegian sky under which they had been written, clear yet deep.

What did it all mean? One lesson incorporated in this accomplished technical exercise emerged clearly near the end: "We had better be silent about that of which we cannot speak." And this realm of the unsayable includes all that really matters. Philosophy no more than science provides us with any answer to the "problems of life." When we have finished philosophizing, the world is as it was; we have not explained it, only described it. Wittgenstein offered some rather cold comfort in the thought that "there are then no questions left, and this itself is the answer. The solution of the problem of life is seen in the vanishing of the problem." There is no more to be said. The book was a kind of exercise in getting this sobering lesson learnt, a clearing of the ground; a ladder, as Wittgenstein wrote, which you kick away as soon as you have used it.

That he now lapsed into silence and appeared to give up his academic career may have been more because of his gloom in the postwar world, his preoccupation with other questions than logical ones, which now appeared trivial. He was deeply affected by Oswald Spengler's fashionably pessimistic *Decline of the West* (*Untergang des Abendlandes*), a popular book just after the war. Following the example of Tolstoy he tried to be a simple schoolteacher in an Austrian village. This aroused Russell's disgust, and he called it "a kind of bogus humility which made him prefer peasants to educated men." It is clear that Wittgenstein in the end found the peasants, or at any rate their children, as disillusioning as the educated men. (He was once accused of using excessive physical force on a student.) He seriously considered becoming a monk, living for a time in a monastery where he served as gardener. Between 1920 and 1928 he sampled these avenues to personal and social salvation, including an investigation of the revolutionary regime in Russia that nonetheless failed to convert him to Communism. He discharged some of his creative energies by designing a house for his sister in Vienna. He also dabbled in sculpture. He inherited his father's money and gave most of it away (not however to the poor!).

This period of withdrawal was followed by a return, as Arnold J. Toynbee would have been pleased to note.[3] Between 1926 and 1928 Wittgenstein engaged in some discussions with members of the Vienna Circle, a group of philosophers who had constituted themselves a movement. They were heirs of Mach and Frege, Logical Positivists whose interest was in a scientific philosophy. Carnap, Schlick, Neurath and others of this group aggressively pressed the attack on metaphysics. True knowledge of the world can come only from empirical observation; *a priori* reasoning produces only tautologies (analytical truths, rearrangements of given knowledge). Therefore the proper function of philosophers is to be helpful to scientists. In a rather Victorian manner they looked forward to science conquering the world at the expense of religion and metaphysics. Their contribution was to be the creation of a logical language, replacing the antiquated and sloppy terminology of everyday speech. The attack on words and sentences that cannot be verified experimentally struck at all manner of vague abstractions. Theologians, someone said, accustomed to being accused of error found it disconcerting to be told they were talking gibberish. The *Wiener Kreis* looked politically leftward, though not as far as Moscow (Lenin had furiously denounced Mach as an "idealist"). One of their group was associated with the short-lived Communist regime of 1919 in Munich.

Carnap and company greatly admired the *Tractatus*, which they construed as supporting their position. Some of Wittgenstein's points seemed to do so. He assumed that there exists an external reality to which language can be made to correspond. Agreeing with Russell that the world is like a bucket of shot rather than a ball of wax, i.e., that it consists of a multitude of separate, atomistic facts, the *Tractatus* appeared to say that propositions can be formulated to match these ultimate "states of affairs." To be sure, a proposition cannot always express the logical forms of external states of affairs, but it can show, depict, or mirror them. This intriguingly subtle point of Wittgenstein's introduced a gap between thought and reality that would later grow into a chasm; but in the *Tractatus* he seemed to agree with the Vienna school in arguing that we can frame a language that will correspond to nature, rather like a map pictures the roads we drive over.

In his talks with the Vienna circle Wittgenstein startled them by preferring to discuss poetry, and they discovered that he really didn't agree with them. In 1932 he said "I used to think there was a direct link between language and reality. I no longer think so." How could we know? We cannot get outside our language; we are its prisoners. In what except language could we talk about the relation between language and the world? How can I picture the relationship between a picture and reality? Something like Heisenberg's interference principle appeared here to set a limit to our knowledge. Rather than language mirroring the world, it may be that the world mirrors our language: its structure, its rules constitute a self-contained system that largely determines the way we see the world. Words derive their meaning less from their correspondence to objects in the external world than from the way they are used in a system of language. The meaning of "green," for example, is determined by its relation to the other names we use for colors, and ultimately to the whole structure of the language (the way the category "color" fits into it.) We may reflect that people know as many colors as their language has names for them; the apparent color-blindness of Homer is explained by the paucity of color terms in the early Greek language. "A name functions as a name only in the context of a system of linguistic and non-linguistic activities."

Wittgenstein wrote nothing further because there seemed to be nothing to say. Ethics was all-important, but it lay beyond the reach of intellectual analysis. Explanation does not dispel mystery: "It is not how things are in the world that is mystical but THAT it exists." In his Spenglerian and Tolstoyan mood of the 1920s Wittgenstein was inclined to disparage Western science and rationalism. "Man has to waken to wonder"; science is a way of putting him to sleep. In this he surprisingly agreed with the philosopher whose direct opposite he was often taken to be, Martin Heidegger. An important influence on him was the Bengali poet and seer Rabindranath Tagore, one of the first of those visiting gurus from the East who earned good lecture fees castigating Westerners for their materialism. Wittgenstein seems to have been extremely susceptible to religious messages presented by imaginative writers such as Tolstoy and Tagore; prone, indeed, to be carried away by trendy enthusiasms in a way that is odd in so critical an intellect. (Karl Marx had the same trait.) It is by no means clear that the poet or novelist is necessarily any better as a guide to life than the philosopher or scientist. Nevertheless his intense spiritual concern, both for himself and for his war-shattered civilization, was one of the qualities that made Wittgenstein so impressive.

Wittgenstein came back to philosophy in 1928 after listening to a lecture by the Dutch mathematician Brouwer, according to the standard account. Brouwer founded mathematics on intuitive knowledge: there is something printed in the human mind which causes all of us to agree spontaneously to certain sequences and relationships. Doubtless Wittgenstein found this suggestion both provocative and hopelessly vague, much in need of refinement. But the reason for his return to his professional life as a philosopher related to his own personal development and to the general movement of Western thought; the shell-shocked 'twenties were about to give way to the "committed" 'thirties. For most intellectuals this meant a pinkish if not red tinge of political activism. Wittgenstein saw through the shallowness of that route, but he was ready in his own way to rejoin the human race, or at any rate that small portion of it that gathered at the universities. His faith in common people had suffered a severe setback! But at the universities he turned away in disgust, too, from the professional word-mongers.

He returned to Cambridge, submitted the *Tractatus* as his dissertation, and was awarded the Ph.D. in a rather unusual manner, Russell and Moore doing the honors. He lectured at Oxford during the 1930s, returning to Cambridge to take Moore's chair in 1939. As an academic personage he proved as unclubbable as ever, taking no part in the games of the profession (doubtless he found them interesting as social customs, "life forms") and becoming unpopular with most of his fellow dons at the university—by tradition an intensely communal life—though he formed close friendships with a few, sometimes unlikely personalities, as with the literary critic F. R. Leavis. He had little respect for his fellow philosophers, it need hardly be said. In his leisure time he read detective stories (like Russell, who had an insatiable appetite for them as mental relaxers) and went to movies. But he worked hard in the 1930s. What was finally published after his death in 1953 as the key book called *Philosophical Investigations* was derived from material he dictated between 1933 and 1935. Like Freud, who had reached his zenith between 1900 and 1905, Wittgenstein in his early forties was clearly in his creative prime. He had ceased being silent; that he published nothing to speak of was owing to his inability to produce anything systematic. The numerous volumes published since his death are in the form of notebooks, "remarks," conversations, lecture notes, or transcripts. This was fitting with his temperament but also with the character of his new philosophical direction.

It has been long customary to distinguish the second Wittgenstein from the first. (Today, Wittgenstein specialists are inclined to identify a third, or a fourth . . .) Word spread in the 1930s that he was creating a new philosophy. Publication in 1953, soon after his death, of *Philosophical Investigations* surprised people accustomed to thinking of him as a positivist. More mature consideration concluded that there was less difference between the earlier and later work than it seemed. Nevertheless there was certainly a pronounced shift of emphasis. Whereas the Logical Positivists had focused on devising a logical language, able to match the real world from its most basic building blocks on up and thus serve as a tool of scientific progress, the later Wittgenstein saw no way of connecting language (or mathematics, logic, any form of expression) with the external world. We are the prisoners of our language, and can know only it. But it is useful to do that. We can (in his term) play consistent language games; avoid confusion, and the flawed communication (hence flawed human relations) that goes with it. We can examine the problems that bother people, problems small and large, and show that they almost always rest on some inconsistent use of language. The value of straightening out these verbal tangles is more for humans than for the cause of natural science. Wittgenstein's interest in psychology increased.

Anyone who has listened to some political or moral argument, the sort that goes on every day, not the least in the press, and has witnessed angry people end the discussion by shouting incoherently at each other, can understand the need for a philosopher like Wittgenstein. It is true that the arguers may not have the patience or wit to listen to such a person; nevertheless this philosopher would insist that all terms be used consistently, in the context of a single "language game." For words take their meaning from the larger structure of language of which they form a part. Ultimately, Wittgenstein came to realize, this language structure is a part of a pattern of culture, in the context of which it forms its meanings; it is a "form of life." (If a lion could talk, we could not understand him, Wittgenstein observed.) There are many different such language games or sub-games. Our speech contains a vast number (a "prodigious diversity" Wittgenstein says) of overlapping languages within the larger one, like a rope made up of tightly wound fibers. Confusion is engendered by "category errors" in jumping from one to another, as if a bridge player should call out "I'm going to castle" instead of leading a card, or "check" instead of "double." The problem with our attempts to think straight, according to Wittgenstein, is something like this: Everybody thinks there is one big game going on, with a single set of rules, whereas in fact the universe of human communication is made up of many smaller games, each with somewhat different rules; and people keep moving about constantly and at random from one table to another.

The philosopher should take language as it is, not try to invent a new one. Our given language is deeply rooted in the common culture, the life-form, redolent of all its values and historical experiences. Ordinary language is the only language there is; it is vain to think of inventing a purer, ideal one, for this would still be cast in terms of our language. This language is however a confused tangle of all sorts and levels of usages, and if we want to think clearly about any question we must untangle it. When this difficult task is performed (we must go through every motion that caused the tangle, unravelling countless hard knots) we normally find, Wittgenstein insisted, that the difficulty disappears. Most arguments are really non-arguments, which are seen to be meaningless when terms are defined. For example, "Can machines think?" is a question that turns entirely on what meaning we give to "machine" and "think."[4] When we clarify these terms, we can state in what sense one might say that machines can think, and in what sense they cannot; the problem as such would vanish. One could, in principle at least, probably do the same for more urgent and passionate issues, such as "Is abortion murder?" or "Is capitalism unjust?"

Of course, the ghost of Sigmund Freud (or Karl Marx) might rise to say that such arguments are not merely cerebral, but have emotional roots that defy intellectual solutions of any sort. Still, there is some similarity between Freudian efforts to go back over the skein of early experiences and memories to relieve anxieties and this Wittgensteinian project of resolving mental confusion by linguistic analysis. Subsequently, a fruitful union between Freudian and linguistic analysis was developed by Jacques Lacan and Jürgen Habermas. Freud's contribution may be viewed as a communications theory. The analyst helps the patient decipher distorted communication within himself, and between himself and other people. There is much support for such a view in the daily reports of juvenile crime, suicide, drug addiction, mental breakdown; "we couldn't communicate with them," "she had something to say but couldn't say it," "he wanted to make a statement," etc. are common reactions from those people close to these innumerable tragedies. Social pathology is at least partly a crisis of communication.

"Ordinary language" is both more trivial and more significant than logical language. Bertrand Russell, increasingly estranged from his one-time friend and student, was scornful of what he construed as a study of "the different ways in which silly people can say silly things." ("I think Wittgenstein's influence has been wholly bad," he wrote in 1959 about his one-time protegé.) Ordinary people do say silly things in everyday speech. But they also touch, albeit confusedly, on questions that are far more important, or at any rate more life-related, than the questions logicians and scientists discuss. They bring in language from all kinds of places, from the streets and markets and churches and theaters, from imaginative literature, folklore, and history. Their language is imprecise, but this is no defect unless we insist on using mathematics or strict logic as the paradigm of expression. Words are usable and useful even if not exact, for life is not exact. Reality is often blurred. The light from my reading lamp, Wittgenstein says, is not sharply bounded. Who can say exactly where it stops? Wittgenstein doubtless knew where physics was trending. Sometimes, he notes, what we need is exactly an *in*distinct word or concept. If this is true even in the natural sciences, how much more is it true in the human ones. This tendency to see an irrational universe was probably what put off that inveterate rationalist and optimist Bertrand Russell.

A corollary of the Wittgenstein analysis of language and thought is that we should "ask for the use, not the meaning" of words and sentences; a Wittgenstein dictionary would not give formal definitions of words but would show how they are variously used, in different contexts.[5] That words are like tools is a leading theme in the later Wittgenstein. A book helpful to mechanics does not attempt to frame a definition of, say, a wrench, but illustrates different wrenches in their different applications. In fact we tend not to have books about wrenches as such, but about kinds of machinery, an automobile for example, in which wrenches and other tools appear as means to build or repair.

Wittgenstein offers us a feast of specific insights, sharply observed, presented in his tantalizing mixture of the memorable and the obscure. He valued the spontaneous idea, the flash of intuition, not the systematic treatise. He despaired, in the end, of creating any sort of systematic book, producing just "remarks." One of his attempts at imposing some sort of order on his insights took the form of clipping short passages, so that presumably they could be pieced together in different ways experimentally; Wittgenstein would have benefitted greatly, one supposes, from the word processor, not yet available to him of course. But he came to realize that system is a false god.

Some of his interests, picked up and labored over by professional philosophers, seem pedantic, rather in the spirit of Berkeley's remark that philosophers first raise dust and then complain they cannot see. Perhaps these questions are not so irrelevant as they seem. One of them is "private language." Wittgenstein's remarks on this subject reflect his insistence that the meaning of a word is not the object which it names or signifies, but its function in the language as a whole. One prevalent view had been that words refer to what can be known only via the experience of the person speaking; we know "pain," for example, only from having felt it. Wittgenstein is concerned to explain that in fact we do not know the word pain this way. I might howl, but I cannot say "I am in pain" unless I know the language including the use of the word "pain" in this language. Language is never private, only sensations are.

This may be interesting in a technical way, but is not likely to seem very important to most people not writing philosophical papers for a living. Wittgenstein's writings are filled with sometimes cryptic insights of this sort, any number of which have provided and continue to provide matter for doctoral dissertations; this would certainly have amused Ludwig. That professional philosophy was so deeply affected by his jottings is a tribute to the cogency of his thought. But this is not the only area of influence. He has had a curiously strong impact on theology. He was of course a deeply religious person, in the sense of being concerned about meanings that lie deeper than our reason, our senses, our logic can reach. "The sense of the world must lie outside the world." The world is a collection of facts, neither good or bad in themselves, just as they are; "in the world everything is as it is." (Time will say nothing but I told you so, W. H. Auden said in a beautiful poem.) The marvel, Wittgenstein said many times, is not *how* things are in the world, but *that* the world as a whole exists. Meaning must lie outside the world. If it lay within the world, it would be just another part of that collection of contingent facts; self-evidently, he thought, "if there is any value that does have value, it must lie outside the whole sphere of what happens and is the case." Equally clear it is that this value, this meaning, lies beyond thought and expression. One cannot speak about value in logical ways. There *are* experiences in which this supramundane absolute may appear to us: our astonishment that the world exists, that anything should exist; feelings also, Wittgenstein says, of being absolutely safe, or absolutely guilty. These experiences are generally incommunicable, as the mystics have always told us. They show us the limits of language, since language cannot hold them.

From the beginning Wittgenstein had felt the limitations of logical thought, of course; the *Tractatus* is an exercise in determining these limits, finding them severe indeed. The "logical form" of reality as well as language—and why these should match, if they do—seemed to him necessarily hidden from us. For we cannot think about language in any metalanguage; we cannot paint a picture about painting a picture. "Logical form" is the structure that underlies the phenomena, something like Kant's "noumena," which we have no way of accessing by logical propositions. We know by reason that it must exist, but our reason can tell us nothing about it. In mystical experiences, perhaps, we can contact it fleetingly, but then there is no way of putting these experiences into cognitive form.

The gulf that separated Wittgenstein from the seemingly similar Logical Positivists is shown here. Both thought that anything attempting to make meaningful statements about reality beyond those of experimental science is nonsense; but the Logical Positivists said this contemptuously, Wittgenstein respectfully, in awe. They dismissed "metaphysics" as containing nothing worth talking about; he refused to talk about it because it is too great to talk about. That words cannot encompass this domain of the suprarational was for them a sign of its insignificance; for him, of its supreme importance. That is why he was so annoyed at being taken for one of the Vienna Circle, and petulantly read Tagore to them when they wanted to discuss scientific language. "Ethics," he said in a 1930 address, "can be no science. What it says does not add to our knowledge in any sense. But it is a document of a tendency in the human mind which I personally cannot help respecting deeply and I would not for my life ridicule it." Ridiculing ethics as no more than empty emoting was just what the Positivists loved to do.

In his relation to religion Wittgenstein was not far from the existentialists (often taken to be his direct opposite). The similarity is suggested by Wittgenstein's remarks on an old theological argument, whether God is bound by a pre-existing reason, or created that reason arbitrarily—whether God necessarily wills what is good, or the Good is what God willed it to be. Wittgenstein thought the latter position the more profound; he aligned himself, in medieval terms, with the voluntarism of Ockham rather than the rationalism of Aquinas. Sartre, the existentialist, also saw an arbitrary, unconditioned will as the source of values, in his case man's rather than God's. This position saves the omnipotence of God—or man—at the cost of some apparently embarrassing implications: if God had chosen to declare torture, murder, disloyalty, etc. to be good, would they have been? We suspect that both Wittgenstein and Sartre stand here in the shadow of Nietzsche, whose insight was the irrationality of a world that simply *is*, without meaning or explanation, a blind struggle between competing energies.

The enduring significance of Wittgenstein is related to at least three central themes in twentieth-century thought with which he intersects.

The first is the linguistic dimension—the growing awareness that what we think depends on the words we use and that these words, and the way they are organized in language, are arbitrarily given to us. Our categories of thought are largely a byproduct of the Greek language's syntax. Wittgenstein was assuredly not the only thinker working in the field of linguistic structures. Ferdinand Saussure, the Swiss whose deeply influential *Course of General Linguistics* appeared in 1915, was a man of about Freud's age, a generation older than Wittgenstein. Much earlier, in 1873, Fritz Mauthner as a student in Prague had experienced the shattering revelation that we are prisoners of our language, which thinks us. A good deal of modern thought has lain under the impact of this insight, one not entirely new in human thought—nothing is—but new in its extent and intensity. Lévi-Strauss, Jakobson, Chomsky, Barthes, and a host of others would make a vogue of "structuralism" at about the time of Wittgenstein's death (in 1951, several years after his retirement.) But Wittgenstein's contribution to this stream of thought was no slight one. No one else made so fascinatingly clear that the disputes and puzzles that humanity has grappled with through the centuries and often fought and died for are simply traps that language sets for us.

Second, one must place him in the context of the revolt against the dominance of scientific naturalism, the result of which has been the restoration of poetry and religion, the imaginative and mythic realms, to an equal and autonomous role. An odd role for him, one might say, but all the more impressive for that. That poets should denounce the reign of materialism hardly surprises us; philosophers of a mystical or idealist tendency might equally be expected to question the scientist's supremacy.[6] When the keenest logical intellect in the western world did so it was another matter. Wittgenstein's authoritative pronouncement that we can only understand this world by somehow getting outside it rallied the confidence of theologians—this despite the fact he was not himself, in any ordinary sense of the word, a believer. He was a seeker, who knew there is something to find, something that is the most important thing in the world, or rather out of it. Wittgenstein's disciples argue that our human faculties can take us as far in the direction of moral truths as science can in the physical realm: a direct reversal of the venerable view that ethics cannot be "scientific."

To this, one should add that there was something morally bracing about Wittgenstein's absolute integrity, his natural, total disdain not only for material gain but for anything commonplace, any compromise with truth. Only the life of the mind counts, and this at the most exacting level. (He told one of his students who considered becoming a journalist that he had much better be a thief!) One glimpses in him the possibility of modern sainthood.

Finally, Wittgenstein looked forward to the deconstruction tendency that the more recent era has so prominently displayed. His sharply deflating analyses of familiar slogans and creeds exposed the contradictions each of them contains. Wittgenstein also provided the tools which others could use to do so. These tools can probe to the heart of any dogma and show the hollowness at its core. They are all vast tautologies, spinning out a heavy web of deception from some one unexamined, questionable assertion (which is probably self-serving: a grasping for greater power or a cry of desire, pain, or resentment).

So Wittgenstein both undercuts all our faiths and insists that we need one. In this he reflects much of the story of modern humanity. Desperately needing something to believe in, the twentieth-century mind finds nothing that can withstand its formidable scepticism. "We have outgrown our religion, outgrown our political system, outgrown our strength of mind and character," a character of George Bernard Shaw's cried in 1934. "The fatal word NOT has been miraculously inscribed in all our creeds." Nothing that has happened since encourages us to think otherwise. Intellectuals put their faith in the bloody tyranny of Stalin's Russia; some even in Hitler's genocidal National Socialism. After the failure of those disgraceful substitute religions, they decided with Jean-Paul Sartre to erect their faith on nothingness. Since then a host of zany and esoteric spiritual fads, imported or manufactured, have competed for the empty, swept, and garnished soul of Western man. In the end it may be that Ludwig Wittgenstein's path is the one we will have to follow. It is rather like Sigmund Freud's in its austerity and integrity. We are permitted no illusions, we must face the awful questions, and we can expect no easy answers.

Notes

[1] Brian McGuiness, *Wittgenstein, A Life: Young Ludwig, 1889-1921* (1988), p. 221.

[2] For an account of the *Tractatus's* adventures see G. H. von Wright, in his *Wittgenstein* (1982).

[3] Toynbee used the theme of "withdrawal and return" as a pattern of creativity

and growth in his *A Study of History*, vol. 3, in which he looked at some thirty-five famous historical figures, including the Buddha, Thucydides, Confucius, St. Paul, Dante, Machiavelli, Loyola, Immanuel Kant, and Lenin. Toynbee wrote this about the same time as Wittgenstein's return from his period of isolation.

[4] Gilbert Ryle's *The Concept of Mind* (1949) was a celebrated exercise in resolving the ancient issue of mind and body along such lines of linguistic analysis.

[5] Use is clearly not the same thing as meaning. One can know the one without the other. One may know how to use, for instance, "amen" without knowing its meaning, at least precisely. Many words have uses without meanings, e.g. personal names, prepositions, conjunctions.

[6] The most influential "return to religion" philosopher of the early twentieth century was the near-contemporary of Freud, Henri Bergson. Bergson was an enchanting writer but not nearly as rigorous a thinker as Wittgenstein.

JOYCE

ONE of Wittgenstein's fellow Viennese, just a few years older than he, also of the "haute bourgeoisie" and a philosopher as well, was Robert Musil. Musil too had tried his hand at being an engineer, then wrote a dissertation on Ernst Mach and was offered a post under the distinguished philosopher Alexius Meinong. But Musil came to feel that only through creative writing, through the "novel," could he come to grips with the whole of modern experience, and thus by understanding it change it. D. H. Lawrence had the same insight about the same time in England, as did Marcel Proust in France: the novel is "the one bright book of life," as Lawrence said, capable of dealing with humanity in its entirety rather than in bits and pieces, and concretely rather than abstractly. The great modernist novelists were psychologists like Freud (they were all more or less obsessed with sex), but their methods were literary rather than scientific. Their interest was the human personality in a problematical society.

These philosophical novelists of the Lawrence-Proust-Kafka-Musil-Joyce generation have filled a large place in modern thought. They incarnate the revolution in style and thought that has marked the twentieth century. To their readers they seemed to express the modern spirit, the twentieth century consciousness. James Joyce's brother Stanislaus once observed, accurately, that "in our world today, serious literature has taken the place of religion. People go, not to the Sunday sermon, but to literature for enlightened understanding of their emotional and intellectual problems." [1]

The pioneer modernist writers all made their debut between about 1905 and 1910 and reached their creative peak in the ensuing decade or so. Marcel Proust began his vast *Search for Lost Time* in 1906 and worked on it until his death in 1922. Lawrence published that great Oedipal novel *Sons and Lovers* in 1913, then wrote *The Rainbow* and *Women in Love* within the next few years, the master works of an amazingly creative writer, who like Proust and Kafka, died much too young. Joyce was a few years older than Lawrence and a few years younger than Proust; three years younger than Einstein, seven years older than Wittgenstein. Before the publication of his *Ulysses* in 1921–22 made him as notable and notorious as Einstein, the Dublin-born Joyce had published some stories about the city with which he had a love-hate relationship (*Dubliners*, published 1914, though he had written most of it some years earlier), as well as an autobiographical *Portrait of the Artist as a Young Man* and a little poetry, none of which departed much from conventional literary style and form. From a decidedly marginal family, he had left Ireland as a 22-year-old, renouncing and resolving not to serve a church and a country in which he said he did not believe. The *Portrait*, or the part of it in another version published as *Stephen Hero*, was a fairly typical story of adolescent rebellion by the artist or intellectual against his appallingly philistine family, teachers, and surroundings; a story far from new, found in writings such as Samuel Butler's *Way of All Flesh* or the plays of Henrik Ibsen especially dear to the adolescent Joyce.

But a literary revolution was underway, providing the means to give fresh form to the story; an intellectual revolution too, as we know. Literature along with the other arts had turned peculiar before Joyce published *Ulysses*. In 1910 a leading English poet pronounced the verses of young Thomas Stearns Eliot "insane." A couple of years later audiences rioted in Paris and Vienna upon hearing the strange music of Stravinsky and Schoenberg. The Austrian emperor struck a Kokoschka painting with his riding whip! A week-long turmoil in Joyce's own city greeted the performance of a play by J. M. Synge. It was not, as sometimes suggested, just the average man or bourgeoisie who took the new works as an insult and sometimes fought back with physical violence. Quite distinguished writers of the older generation also indignantly repudiated the new art. It seemed shockingly incomprehensible and antisocial.

In 1914 Joyce with his companion Nora (Joyce lived with Nora Barnacle ever since he took her with him from Ireland in 1904, but they were not married until twenty-seven years later) and two small children moved from Trieste, where he had lived most of the time since 1904 (he was in Rome for six months or so during 1906 and 1907), to Zurich. It was there that he wrote most of *Ulysses*. It is engaging to think of that other and very different revolutionary, Lenin, also living in Zurich during these war years. (Einstein had just left.) Joyce's interest in politics was apparently minimal. "Don't talk to me about politics," he once snapped to Stanislaus. "I'm only interested in style." But the overtly apolitical attitude usually conceals a deep and bitter alienation.[2] *Ulysses* was as much a product of the war as many a work explicitly about battle. Homer's hero had been a warrior; Joyce once pointed out that Ulysses invented the tank, after having initially been a draft-dodger. Tennyson's great Victorian poem about the ancient Greek hero has him getting bored with peace after his adventures and embarking again on a last voyage, determined to "drink life to the lees," following knowledge "beyond the utmost bound of human thought." Tennyson thought Ulysses a perfect symbol of Life, and Joyce agreed that he was "the complete man." After the deluge, Western society obviously needed to reinvent man by returning to the sources.

Portions of Joyce's startling book appeared in 1920 in the American avant-garde magazine *Little Review*, a publication banned in Britain after a judge pronounced it incomprehensible as well as immoral, though it is difficult to see how it could have been both. The edition published in 1922 in Paris by another obscure American enterprise (Sylvia Beach's Shakespeare & Co.) was soon an eagerly sought-after collector's item, copies selling for upwards of $300 (in today's money, at least $3,000). Joyce seemed to be remaking language just as Einstein had reshaped the fabric of the universe and Freud the topography of the mind. That *Ulysses* was just as difficult to understand as relativity and psychoanalysis mattered little to the sharply disillusioned, curious postwar "lost" generation. (The relation between Joyce and Einstein appears in a Paris magazine founded in the 1920s by Joyce admirers, *transition* [sic], which announced as its goal "a pan-symbolic, pan-linguistic synthesis in the conception of a four-dimensional universe.")

Response to the widely publicized contraband book was divided about equally between the deeply impressed and the utterly shocked. "Morbid and sickening," "the foulest book that has ever found its way into print" mingled with "the most important expression which this age has found"—T. S. Eliot's judgment—or American critic Edmund Wilson's "a work of high genius which has the effect of making everything else look brassy." Not many informed people today would question the latter two judgments, yet to this day the average man's opinion may be akin to that expressed by a Dublin cabdriver in 1982: "That gobshite they threw out of the country for his dirty writings." The scandalous features of course scarcely detracted from the book's fame. *Ulysses* does not today seem either as shocking or as difficult, not to say incomprehensible, as it then did. By comparison with its sequel, *Finnegans Wake*, it is clarity itself. But at that time it was eye-opening for several reasons. The subject matter is the interior mind, revealed by the technique of "stream of consciousness" or interior monologue (not always; some parts of *Ulysses* are conversational or descriptive in a more traditional way, enlarged by Joyce's extraordinary linguistic gift.) And of course any person's unedited private ruminations are likely to be wandering and disorganized as well as occasionally unspeakable. Joyce's attempt to get at this obscure realm of private thoughts may be compared to Freud's, or to Husserl's "phenomenology," which struggled to find the structure of consciousness itself. It is a parlous and perhaps impossible enterprise. How can we know another mind, from the inside? How can we put into words what lies beneath words? But it is intensely interesting.

A novel feature too was the plot structure of *Ulysses*, which is not a narrative in the usual sense but "nodal," weaving the events through the texture of the book; they bob up again and again like Wagnerian *leitmotifs* but are nowhere narrated in a consecutive manner. We should not ignore the influence of Wagner on Joyce, who was deeply musical; a "seminal influence," as Matthew Hodgart says. Straightforward narrative, doubtless, would have been too boring for Joyce. By putting together bits and pieces of thought and conversation we eventually learn a great deal about the life of Leopold Bloom and his wife Molly, the death of their son, their estrangement since then, Molly's affair with Blazes Boylan, the death and funeral of one of their friends, and many other things. These occurences are archetypal: there is birth, death, eating and drinking, marriage, all the events of life in this one day which is the life of all humanity. There is an entire history of English literature in one chapter, beginning with the confusion of pre-language, in a series of brilliant and amusing imitations of every prose style from Old English on down. The Circe brothel scene combines realism with myth and fantasy. Parts of *Ulysses* etch a vividly realistic picture of Dublin, marvelously reproducing the lingo of the local citizens, in the city where everyone seems able to talk well. A man of vast, almost incredible learning, Joyce was also a master of the common speech, the popular mentality, from which indeed he sprang.

There is in *Ulysses* a curious ambivalence toward these priest-ridden, squalid, besotted, bigotted Dubliners whom the young Joyce had found so horrible, but who seem to represent essential humanity. The story of *Ulysses* is on one level a *Bildungsroman*, taking its place in a long tradition of such stories of a young person's emergence into self-discovery. It is a continuation of *Portrait of the Artist* by other methods. Stephen Dedalus, who is in good part Joyce himself, is a rather troubled young man, from a destitute family, guilt-ridden for refusing to pray at his mother's deathbed; earning little at a teaching job (with indifferent students), he dreams of becoming a great writer but does not quite know how to go about it. He hates Dublin, though this is all he knows to write about. Among other troubles, he has just been ejected from his rooming house for not paying his rent. During the course of the novel he will meditate, debate, carouse, and finally discover a new father; he is to be the Telemachus to Bloom's Ulysses.

But it is the latter who is the chief figure of the novel. Almost all of the interior monologue/stream of consciousness is Bloom's (though the most famous one is reserved for Molly Bloom in the final chapter.) If Stephen Dedalus is Joyce himself, who is the prototype for this modern Ulysses, Leopold Bloom? His wife, Molly, is presumably based on Joyce's Nora, though she denied this; episodes in *Ulysses* mirror known incidents in the personal life of the Joyces. So there must be some of Joyce in Bloom too, but the latter is Jewish, rather non-intellectual, with evidently no literary ambitions or aptitudes (in fact lowbrow tastes), and in other ways, too, quite unlike Joyce. Bloom may well represent the father than James would have liked to have had. Joyce idealized fatherhood, placing it above motherhood—"the madonna which the cunning Italian intellect flung to the mob of Europe." But his own father, the feckless John Joyce, was something of a disappointment.

One possible real-life model for Bloom was Joyce's friend Italo Svevo, pen name of Hector Schmitz, a Hungarian Jew who had settled in the city of Trieste. A minor writer and a wit, a shrewd observer of modernity who translated Freud into Italian, Svevo encouraged Joyce to press on with *Portrait of the Artist as a Young Man*.[3] Leopold Bloom is of Hungarian Jewish ancestry and a migrant to Dublin—a city not unlike Trieste in some ways. The age difference between Joyce and Svevo, the older man by twenty years, is close to that between Stephen Dedalus and Bloom in *Ulysses*. We note also that Svevo's wife was named Livia, a name that will appear in *Finnegans Wake*.

Bloom in any case is an epic figure. Early readers often took him as a satire on modern man: real heroes are no longer possible in our grubby world. Bloom is indeed in some ways overtly a figure of fun. His wife deceives him, he embarrassingly has to relieve himself in public, he carries on a ludicrous flirtation by mail, he has tried to seduce the maid, etc.—the catalog of Bloom's minor idiocies is long. He entertains absurd fantasies of himself as great lover and as hero-statesman. In reality as a small-time commercial salesman he ranks very low in the social hierarchy of Dublin, though obviously as Joyce sees it this is no disgrace. But in fact Bloom is a totally decent man, kind, generous, sensitive, also intelligent and occasionally quite insightful. There is no malice in him, and he exhibits an engaging curiosity about life—there is "something of the scientist" in him and a lot of homely wisdom along with some folkish inanities. He is capable of spiritual grandeur. He comes away from his encounters with a host of Dubliners, including scholars, priests, and public officials as well as whores and drunken soldiers, looking good by contrast, possessing a kind of basic, if awkward, dignity and humanity. In the end we love this strange creature as we can hardly love many of his betters.

Bloom of course is meant to represent far more than himself. Though a vividly realized individual given local habitation on this one day (June 16, 1904) in Dublin, surrounded by its sights, sounds, and events, he is also Everyman. This mythic quality is indicated by making the episodes in Bloom's day correspond to adventures of Homer's Ulysses (Joyce does not name them in chapter titles: you have to know them, a foretaste of the mystification he was to raise to greater heights in *Finnegans Wake*). It is made evident also in many other ways. There is explicit reference to recurrence. Molly is scornful of Leopold using big words she cannot even spell; the leading example is "metempsychosis" ("that word met something with hoses in it and he came out with some jawbreakers about the incarnation. . . . ") So Bloom is Ulysses and Elijah and the Wandering Jew and, as one passage puts it,

> Sinbad the Sailor and Tinbad the Tailor and Jinbad the Jailer and Whinbad the Whaler and Ninbad the Nailer and Finbad the Failer and Binbad the Bailer and Pinbad the Pailer and Minbad the Mailer and Hinbad the Hailer and Rinbad the Railer and Dinbad the Kailer and Vinbad the Quailer and Linbad the Yailer and Xinbad the Phthailer.

Clearly the more than 700 pages of *Ulysses* contain far more than one man could really have done and thought in some sixteen hours. After a famous evening adventure with Gerty MacDowell in the park, Bloom stops by the red light district ("Nighttown") where in the longest and most fantastical chapter he meets Stephen and sees him through a fight with some drunken British soldiers; the two then have a drink with some cabmen and, making their way homeward, discourse about "music, literature, Ireland, Dublin, Paris, friendship, woman, prostitution, diet" and among other things the Roman Catholic church, Jesuit education, and the study of medicine. Yet they seem to arrive at Bloom's house by midnight.

Obviously there is something artificial in the "stream of consciousness" style. No one really thinks to herself continuously in words, as Molly does in her celebrated soliloquy, unless one is very literary and intellectual, which Molly was not; more likely it is in images—pictures, shapes, sounds, or if words, a blur of them not precisely formulated. (Joyce was soon led in this direction.) The sheer virtuosity of this tour de force of literature, the 1600 lines of Molly's unpunctuated sentence, bowls us over and we may willingly suspend our disbelief that this is a real woman's inner mind unrolling before us. But if Molly had actually said all these words to herself it would have taken her several hours, rather than a few minutes before going to sleep. Again, the intent seems to be to verbalize for the human race: Molly is an archetypal woman, a great earth mother or goddess, if not (as many have thought) the Life Force itself. Some female critics have seen projections of masculine fantasy here; could Joyce, a man, really know what women think about? The objection seldom occurred to anyone until recently. Joyce had known Nora intimately for many years when he wrote *Ulysses*, and the unpunctuated style of her letters resembles Molly's mode of expression.

Joyce, like all great literary artists—one of his favorites, Dickens, comes to mind—invents a world and makes us believe in it; then it is accepted as "reality." The world Joyce invented in *Ulysses* contains his own (hardly typical) experiences as a native of Dublin; it also contains all sorts of ideas and knowledge that the scholar-writer James Joyce had absorbed in his omnivorous reading. The larger goal of the work into which Joyce put so many laborious hours is simply this: to invent a world, to create a work of art. It was a goal found widely among the *fin de siècle* writers of Europe and America. It was based partly on their rejection of the existing social world as "a hideous society," vulgar, crude, materialistic, selfish, dominated by "bourgeois" philistines. The artist-intellectual profoundly alienated from this real world appears at this time as a strongly recognizable type. The Symbolist poets who flourished just before Joyce and who strongly influenced him—Mallarmé, especially—of whom it was said that they could neither accept nor transform reality (the utopian dreams of the socialists seemed to them boring as well as naive) had dared to invent a wholly different world of the imagination, making it as bizarre as possible.

The other part of the equation is the artist-intellectual's own highly developed consciousness based on immersion in literature. The young Joyce did indeed bathe himself in books. His brother says he read at the National Library every evening until it closed at ten. Supplementing his Jesuit-taught studies of the classics, he read Tolstoy and Turgenev and D'Annunzio, Verlaine and Maeterlinck and Sudermann, as well as his idolized Ibsen. He copied out and committed to memory long passages from Carlyle, Ruskin, Newman, and Macaulay, the Victorian classics. He was probably more a master of the Western intellectual tradition than any of the other figures we have dealt with, though the others were no slouches. This was perhaps chiefly why he did not like the Irish literary renaissance, so potent a force in his own time in Ireland, and why he left Ireland and partly hated it: he rejected Irish nationalism's attempt to substitute the Gaelic language and tradition for the European.

Joyce's fascination with style and all his accumulated lore appears in his books, which are attempts to come to terms with the totality of life. Of course, Joyce came to feel that most "literature" was too divorced from the reality of life in the grubby streets of "dear dirty Dublin," the society he knew. He must include the other side too, with its popular songs and drunken husbands, barflies and barmaids, prostitutes and beggars—as the realistic writers like Zola, Ibsen, Hamsun, and George Moore had tried or were trying to do.

To Stanislaus he once said, after his brother had told him he didn't believe in the Roman Catholic mass, "Don't you think there is a certain resemblance between the mystery of the Mass and what I'm trying to do? I mean that I am trying in my poems to give people some kind of intellectual pleasure or spiritual enjoyment by converting the bread of everyday life into something that has a permanent artistic value of its own . . . " A religion for modern man provided by the artist: Richard Wagner had had the same dream.

After *Ulysses*, Joyce embarked upon a strange literary adventure which was to occupy him the rest of his life, some seventeen years. Certainly the opus he eventually titled *Finnegans Wake* (it is still frequently misspelled, with an apostrophe) was and remains "one of the strangest books ever to have gained admittance to the sphere of criticism," as critic J. I. M. Stewart remarks. His brother, his wife, his patient benefactor Harriet Weaver, and indeed almost everybody who knew him thought he had, to put no finer point on it, gone off his rocker. (Stanislaus refused to accept a copy of *Finnegans Wake* when it was finally published in 1939.) The "Work in Progress," as it was initially known (portions of it being printed in *transition* from time to time) aroused excitement among a small band of devotees but mystified everyone else. Meanwhile *Ulysses* went its controversial way, finally winning out over the censorship to reach a wide public only in the 1930s. (Except for small printings in 1922–23 most copies of which were confiscated, the first American edition was published by Random House in 1934, the first English one by Bodley Head in 1936–37.) The public was engaged in absorbing *Ulysses*, far from an easy task. The rumor that Joyce was writing another and far more difficult book left them fairly cold.

Finnegans Wake is written in a language which seems to bear only a tangential relation to English. Open the book to any page and you will find apparent nonsense, such as

Thank you. Sir, kindest of bottleholders and very dear friend, among our hearts of steel, froutiknow, it will befor you, me dare beautiful young soldier, winninger nor anyour of rudimental moskats, before you go to mats, you who have watched your share with your sockboule sodalists on your buntad nogs at our love tennis squats regatts . . .

If we reflect that "froutiknow" may be a speeded-up "for ought I know," while "rudimental moskats" comes close to "regimental muskets," and if we happen to know that Hearts of Steel was an Irish revolutionary society, we still are hardly out of the woods and are left with the further question of why Joyce did not write these words in the usual way instead of disguising them (we have "befall," "Mass," "bended knees" also in distorted form, though perhaps recognizable). The above passage is well above average in comprehensibility by *Wake* standards. This sentence, however, continues on for twenty-one lines, not getting any easier. It is an important moment in the story, when the father figure HCE finally confesses his voyeurism (observed by two soldiers) in Phoenix Park, an event symbolic of man's original sin and fall. Again, at random from the 628 pages,

> Will ate evereadayde saumone like a boyne alive O. The tew cherripickers, with their Catheringnettes, Lizzy and Lissy Mycock, from Street Flesh-shambles, were they moon at aube with hespermun and I their covin guardient, I would not know how to contact such gretched youngsteys in my ways from Haddem or any sistersees or heiresses of theirn, claiming by, through or under them. Ous of their freiung pfann into myne foyer.

Again, a little Trivial Pursuit knowledge British-style will help, e.g., that the Cherry Pickers were Prince Albert's Hussars and that there is a Fishamble Street in Dublin, while a catherinette in France is a young unmarried woman. We obviously have again the two soldiers and some girls HCE is anxious to deny he ever knew. The fleshshambles pun may strike us as clever. But why the obfuscations?

Curious indeed! One reason for the gibberish is that we are in dream-land. *Finnegans Wake* is a dream, and Joyce is trying to simulate or recount the interior monologue of the dreamer much as he did in *Ulysses* for one awake. Because in dreams we are nearer to the unconscious mind with its mythic images and archetypes, where individual identity dissolves in a sea of words, *Finnegans Wake* is more transpersonal than *Ulysses*; we have many foreign words, in a dozen languages, and a host of reincarnations. The dreamer is ostensibly a tavern keeper named Humphrey Chimpden Earwicker, but he is, even more than Leopold Bloom, the entire human race: Haveth Childers Everywhere, also Howth Castle and Environs, i.e., the city of Dublin, metonymically the whole world. Frequently he is King Mark of the Tristan and Isolde legend, Parnell, the great Irish politician, St. Patrick, Jonathan Swift, the Duke of Wellington, a Russian general, as well as Adam and Moses and Caesar, and of course Finn MacCool, legendary Irish hero, along with Tim Finnegan from a popular Irish song. He is even, as H_2CE_3, a chemical formula. One of his names, Huges Caput Earlyfouler, evokes medieval French and German kings (Hugh Capet, Henry the Fowler) as well as big heads and untrained infants. HCE is also partly his twin sons, who themselves appear in a variety of guises during the dream. Themes from *Ulysses* are carried over into *Wake*. In the park at twilight Bloom spied on the undergarments, willingly revealed, of Gerty MacDowell; HCE's sin, the chief node of *Finnegans Wake*, was something similar, committed in Phoenix Park. Bloom's incestuous thoughts about his daughter Millie resemble HCE's desire for Isolde/Isabel. The unsatisfactory state into which Leopold and Molly's love life had deteriorated (evidently matching the real-life situation of James and Nora) is duplicated in HCE and his wife Anna Livia Plurabelle. Stephen Dedalus, i.e. Joyce himself, in *Finnegans Wake* has become one of the brothers, Shem, who is contrasted with the non-poetic, practical, and rather stupid Shaun, a character partly drawn from James's brother (a reason for Stanislaus's rejection of the book). Nature themes play a larger part in the later work. If HCE is a geographic area, ALP is the river Liffey. Shem and Shaun seem to represent antithetical philosophical principles: spirit and body, yin and yang, the dualism in Giordano Bruno's thought. They are also, of course, the artist-intellectual versus the bourgeois-practical man; in Freudian terms, the pleasure versus the reality principle.

Dante, Bruno, Freud, Jung (and Morton Prince, the American student of multiple personality)—the list of those whose ideas Joyce made use of is a long one. The most notable is Giambattista Vico, the remarkable eighteenth century Neapolitan thinker whose thought became widely known only in the nineteenth century. Largely due to Benedetto Croce, Vico was much in vogue when Joyce was growing up. Georges Sorel, whom Joyce admired[4] wrote on Vico in the 1890s. Vico was a predecessor of Hegel and Marx, a philosopher who first clearly glimpsed the fact that man makes himself in history by the use of language. Vichian imagery permeates *Finnegans Wake*. Vico's cycles of history, his *corso, ricorso*, appear in the endless circle of the novel (the last lines feed into the first so that we start all over again, as in Nietzsche's Eternal Return). "The Vico road goes round and round to meet where terms begin" (p. 452). The roll of thunder that Vico placed at the end of one age and the beginning of another appear in *Finnegans Wake* as hundred-letter words (e.g. Ullhodturdenweirmudgaardgring-nirurdrmolnirfenrirlukkilokkbaugimandodrrerinsurtkrinm-gernrackinarockar!)

Let us take another example from *Finnegans Wake* in order to answer the question of what qualities the style adds to the thought. The last chapter contains a passage which admittedly is more directly philosoph-ical than usual, and also apparently an intrusion of Joyce himself, the author speaking. But for that very reason it seems a good test of the *Wake*'s extraordinary style as a medium able to say more than could be said in straightforward prose:

You mean to see we have been hadding a sound night's sleep? You may so. It is just, it is just about to, it is just about to rolywholyover. Svapnas-vap. Of all the stranger things that ever not even in the hundrund and badst pageans of unthowsent and wonst nice or in eddas and oddes bokes of tomb, dyke and hollow to be have happened! The untireties of livesliv-ing being the one substrance of a streamsbecoming. Totalled in toldteld and teldtold in tittletell tattle. Why? Because, graced be Gad and all giddy gadgets, in whose words were the beginnings, there are two signs to turn to, the yest and the ist, the wright side and the wronged side, feeling aslip and wauking up, so an, so farth. Why? On the sourdsite we have the Moskiosk Djinpalast with its twin adjacencies, the bathouse and the ba-zaar, allahallahallah, and on the sponthesite it is the alcovan and the ro-segarden, boony noughty, all puraputhry. Why? One's apurr apuss a story about brid and breakfedes and parricombating and coushcouch but others is of tholes and oubworn buyings, dolings and chafferings in heat, contest and enmity. Why? Every talk has his stay, vidnis Shavarsanjivana, and all-a-dreams perhapsing under lucksloop at last are through. Why? It is a sot of swigswag, systomy dystomy, which everabody you ever anywhere at all doze. Why? Such me.

The long night's dream of Earwicker alias Finnegan alias King Mark alias Everyman (or perhaps Joyce himself?) is coming to an end, and in the above passage Joyce is saying maybe one person's dream is some-how the same as all of human history, "the untireties of livesliving." Our collective unconscious contains all the myths and stories of the total human experience—an idea which obviously underlies the novel we have just read. "Why is every dream an epic of the history of man, why does each of us contain the mosaic of the entire pattern in the chaotic splinters that form our dreams?"[5] To explain this Joyce reverts to the dualistic philosophy so central to his conception of the cosmos. If life as a whole, like each individual's life, is an alternation of dream and awakening, these two modes are opposites and opposed, though also linked. One is a realm of action, commerce, war—"heat, contest and enmity" (repeating the HCE initials). (We think of Freud's reality principle, or Max Weber's rationalization and disenchantment, or Marx's eternal bourgeoisie.) The other is a softer and prettier world of sensual delights.[6] The dualism also seems to prevail between the private realm (family, marriage, not without its struggles, "parricombating") and the public one. Each has its place in the scheme of things, a perpetual ebb and flow, yin and yang, eternal recurrence. Who knows why this is so?

This passage of Joyce contains a bit of Sanskrit and a reference to the muezzin's call in Islamic religion, as well as some disguised Italian ("boony naughty" = buona notte) and other allusions which are a part of world history or literature; and it refers as *Finnegans Wake* always does to other motifs in the dense interconnections within the novel itself: e.g., "lucksloop" is the village of Leixlip on the Liffey near Dublin which means "salmon leap" and is a recurring geographic image. Every word may be analyzed to find deeper levels of meaning. Our dreams are both "through" (Finnegans are waking, we are into a new phase of history) and "true". "Such me" means "search me!" (slang, "blessed if I know") but also, perhaps, "such is the way I am/the world is" or even "search me" in the non-colloquial sense: look inside myself/ yourself, the answer may be there somewhere.

We will certainly be moved to admire the breathtaking verbal wizardry of conjoint meanings: "falling asleep" as "feeling a slip," the West and the East as the Yes and the Is, the two sides as not Right and Wrong but Wright (made?) and Wrong*ed*. Everybody does/doze, recapping the awake and the dreaming. And so on (or an). When we reflect that this packing in of meanings has gone on for more than 600 pages, we can only gasp in wonder at the immensity of the achievement, as a sheer tour de force of language. The question remains, what advantage is there in saying it in so disguised and difficult a fashion, rather than in simple, direct English?

The advantage, no doubt, of art and metaphor. One of the chief philosophical underpinnings of *Finnegans Wake* is Joyce's conviction, derived from Vico as well as from many contemporaries such as Nietzsche and Bergson and Sorel, that modern life is decadent because it is overly rationalized and needs to return to the spontaneity of primitive instinct. *Finnegans Wake* is of course a dream. The dream world to Joyce, as the above passage seems to say, is the softer world, the Oriental world, a fantasy opposed to the materialistic bustle of everyday existence in the modern West. It is also the sourd (deaf) side, deaf to the sounds of the awake world. It may thus be viewed as a utopian alternative to a depressing reality. But Joyce also thought it could be a source of the language renewal, the *ricorso*, which his beloved Vico stressed. In dreams we may rediscover the lost mentality of early humanity when words were magic and poetry was natural, before the rational and the useful drove religion and art into the margins of existence.

Some have wondered how Vico thought we could get back to that ancient time before the senses and the instincts were replaced by intellect and reflection, and heroes gave way to businessmen. The Neapolitan writer suggested that there is a cycle; we simply exhaust one phase and then, with a roll of thunder, revert back to where we began. But clearly this is hard to believe. We cannot really extinguish everything in consciousness this way. Unless civilization is totally wiped out in some enormous physical catastrophe, something must remain of the earlier ages, and people cannot really be savages again. They can at best only pretend to be. But in dreams and imaginative life we can restore contact with that earlier mentality and thus renew ourselves spiritually.

Ulysses and *Finnegans Wake* constitute achievements so immense that they cannot be ignored. Those whom they intensely annoy are compelled to concede their stature.[7] One can dismiss Joyce perhaps as a manic genius; the madhouses are full of idiot-savants, often with uncanny special aptitudes. The kind of massive logomania that Joyce possessed was, unfortunately for any such thesis, combined with an equally impressive mastery of the world's literary and intellectual inheritance. He knew the classics, he knew the lore of many other cultures, he knew languages, and he knew some science and mathematics. He had absorbed Freud and Marx and Jung and all that. And one of the marvels of the two great "novels" (it seems wrong to call them that, for they are also encyclopedias, epics, and poems) is that they encompass low as well as high culture. To catch all the allusions you have to have some knowledge of the culture not only of Dublin pubs and music-halls but of contemporary American low culture. Comic strips, popular songs, movies—Mutt and Jeff, "Yes We Have No Bananas," "The Man Who Broke the Bank at Monte Carlo" and a hundred other fragments of the inane and incessantly changing cultural world of twentieth-century ur-ban mass-man are as ubiquitous in Joyce's books as Celtic legend and Irish politics. There is a television sketch (verbivocovisual) in *Finnegans Wake*, rather precocious for someone writing in the 1930s.

Joyce once told a friend that "it isn't I who am writing this crazy book, but you, and you, and you," as he pointed about him in the café. He was trying to put into words or into some conceptual framework what T. S. Eliot called "the immense panorama of futility and anarchy which is contemporary history." The writer, Shem, does not receive any special sympathy from Joyce. He is as flawed as his tone-deaf brother. "Shem was a sham and a low sham." "You have reared your disunited kingdom on the vacuum of your own most intensely doubtful soul," his brother scolds him. "Do you hold yourself for some god in the manger . . . ?" "Sniffer of carrion, premature gravedigger," Shem as seen by Shaun is surely much the way Joyce saw him; Joyce participated in that revulsion from morbid egoism that paradoxically afflicted many European intellectuals even as they explored the frontiers of deep sub-jectivity. They both loathed and were fascinated by "decadence," the state of modern society marked by dissolution of social and spiritual unity. Joyce wanted to escape the trap of solipsism to engage the entire social world. Hence the attempt to create a language that would tran-scend individuality.

Few lines pass without a stunning portmanteau word or pun. The days of the week in *Finnegans Wake* include Comeday, flyday, sendday, thirstay (thirstay mournin.) The days of an obviously bad week, such as we all have, included Moansday, Tearsday, Wailsday, Frightday, Shat-terday. After this who can be altogether happy with any straightforward calendar? One finds himself giving the days new names: my girlfriend chewed me out on Shrewsday, my dog is happy on Setterday. Fre-quently Joyce parodies or puns on familiar bromides: the waste of all peaceable worlds, a coming offence sends its shudders before. A kind of boredom with the Same Old Language obviously infected Joyce, to the extent that he could almost never use the accepted word or phrase. And why not? The restless, neophilic modern has to change styles con-stantly in dress, in design, in ideas, role models. Youngsters invent new words and phrases every year; empires of slang arise in ghettoes or on California beaches. With the "shoutmost shoviality" Joyce affirmed life and parodied it simultaneously.

"Its prose is the prose of the world" says one Joyce student and admirer, John Bishop, of *Finnegans Wake*. It is Everybody's. One might object: But is it not therefore nobody's? Who can be everybody? Only James Joyce. And despite Bishop's claim, in the end even Joyce cannot stand in place of all humanity. He is after all just one time-bound Irish consciousness, however extraordinarily rich a one. In fact he makes this evident; Everybody is clearly an Irishman, first and foremost. Almost all the principal stories and motifs in *Finnegans Wake* are drawn from Irish songs and legends and history, or from a close neighbor in England or Cornwall. That foreign phrases are frequently thrown in does not alter the essential English language basis of the work. And the single most helpful aid to understanding Finneganese is a knowledge of Irish popular songs, verses, jokes, and folk tales, together with the politics of Joyce's own nation in his own time. ("The Irish are the most civilized race in Europe," Joyce wrote, even as he was running away from them.)

To understand *Finnegans Wake* one would have to duplicate Joyce's consciousness, a daunting enterprise. It is safe to say no one can do that. Decades of textual analysis enlisting the talents of hundreds of experts (our university English departments, it is comforting to know, contain numerous well-paid scholars who mostly know only something about the Joyce novels) have resulted in but a partial comprehension of the *Wake*. A handful of people around the world can claim to approach a comprehension of it. Joyce assured himself of immortality by writing a book so difficult that it will take centuries to unravel all its meanings. Many thousands more become intrigued and become Joyceists in some sense. Several thousand of them clogged the streets of Dublin on Bloomsday, June 1982, the hundredth anniversary year of Joyce's birth, reenacting scenes from *Ulysses* to the amazement of the natives. These enthusiasts were not all college professors.

How many others have been struck so forcefully by some phrase or image of *Ulysses* or *Finnegans Wake* that it significantly altered their personality and their life, even their choice of mate, career, or leisure time activity? No one knows, of course. Everabuddy or knowboddy.

Beyond all questions of deciphering meaning, the novels radiate an attitude or life-sense which can rub off on those innumerable people who have browsed in them. The glow that hangs over them is a warm, intoxicating one. A great vitality, an exuberance for life combines with a rich awareness of all humanity's words and aspirations. It is an exalting, ennobling influence, ultimately a kind of divine madness. It exposes the absurdity of our paradoxical cosmos while delighting in it. No one who has really tasted this Joycean liquor is likely to be content with anything else. He must return to those mystifying books for annual refreshment.

We might suggest finally that these books have a strangely democratic quality. Joyce began as a characteristically antisocial artist of the era he grew up in, the years around the turn of the century. The standard type was a denizen of little cafés who drank opium or absinthe, cried "I detest the mob!", and created incomprehensible, experimental poems or pictures or compositions to spite the bourgeoisie. From these esthetic rebels emanated what C. P. Snow reproachfully declared to be nothing but "a scream of horror" against the mainstream society. Joyce, fleeing his native city and always living a kind of rootless artist's existence (to the immense psychic distress of his children, incidentally) was in some ways as alienated as any. Everything about Dublin is horrible in Joyce's early work, *Dubliners*. But in *Ulysses* we are not so sure. Carl Jung thought that the book was a satire on modern life, an essay on its emptiness: Nothing happens, to nobodies, nowhere, and that is the point. Few Joyce students accept this view. Bigots and fools do inhabit Bloom's city, but by no means all his characters are detestable. A love of humanity with all its foibles shines through.

There is a democratic element in interior monologue. We enter the consciousness of Everyman, where the same basic archetypes dwell— "interior monologue asserts a total intimacy which must preclude 'distance.'"[8] Social rules and prejudices no longer figure. The mind of the petty Jewish salesman Bloom is as rich and full as anyone's and basically like everyone's. In any case it is there, and the object of *Ulysses* is to display it, as it is—the miracle of a single human consciousness. In *Finnegans Wake* Joyce made the daring claim that somehow the whole of human history may be found in the individual consciousness—almost anyone's.

The eponymous Tim Finnegan is the comic hero of an Irish ballad who gets drunk and falls down dead but comes to life again at his wake when somebody throws whiskey on him. Finnegans wake (no apostrophe). So do we all. The Vico road goes round and round, life endlessly repeats itself. The life force does not exhaust itself. Among the recurring symbols in *Finnegans Wake* is the date 1132. Eleven is the number that starts over again, the first repeated number, repeated yet new. Thirty two is the Galilean rate of acceleration in free fall. Humanity falls over and over again, but always rises.

We are all equally guilty and equally pardonable. "Guilty but fellows culpows!" is HCE's final plea. Puns on "felix culpa," happy fault, the fortunate fall of Christian theology—in the end Adam's sin was not a bad but a good thing because it led to redemption—run throughout the book. Here it is mixed into "fellow culprits." The main theme of *Finnegans Wake*, it seems, is a healing of the family's (for which of course read the human family's) schisms and quarrels. Shem and Shaun quarrel bitterly; both rebel against the father. ALP is jealous of her daughter. But there is reconciliation in the common consciousness; these people after all are really only thoughts in the universal mind of the dream world, and sometimes they even interchange or blend.[9]

In the end each of his readers must decide if Joyce has created the supreme work of human genius or a monstrous bore and failure. Anyone who persists with *Finnegans Wake* will probably think many times that both of these things are true. He may turn back to *Ulysses* with relief; but then that great book may become so familiar to him that he must try again the deeper waters of *Finnegans Wake*. The word wizardry will hold him in thrall as an addict, making all other writers look cheap and paltry. How shagsome all and beastful! The annamation of evabusies, the livlianess of her laughings, such a plurity of bells! Alla tingaling pealabells! Old Finncoole, he's a mellow old saoul when he swills with his fuddlers free! Here be trouts culponed for ye and salmons chined and sturgeons tranched, sanced capons, lobsters barbed. Such a boyplay! What tyronte power! Bravose!

Joyce died younger, not quite fifty-nine, than any of our other figures, and the last years of his life were somewhat tragic, marred chiefly by the mental illness of his daughter and his daughter-in-law. Joyce was by nature a happy person who loved music, on occasion swilled rather too much, and liked to dine out with his friends. He enjoyed in the main a happy marriage with the delightful Nora—who, unlike Sartre's Simone, contributed nothing at all to his literary work but supplied him with an essential humanity that, one may argue, is the underlying feature of his great novels. She was Molly Bloom and Anna Livia Plurabelle and that generalized Life Force that Joyce thought so essentially feminine. But Joyce had more than his share too of the selfishness of the artist (who, George Bernard Shaw said, "will let his wife starve, his children go barefoot, his mother drudge for a living at seventy, sooner than work at anything but his art"). The perpetual changes of residence doubtless contributed to the children's psychoemotional problems. Tragedy of a larger sort struck in the last year of his life; the German conquest of France forced the Joyces to flee to Switzerland amid great confusion, leaving daughter Lucia in a French sanitarium (she eventually arrived in England). The stomach ulcer that led to Joyce's death must have owed something to these drastic disturbances.

But his life work was finished. It is a legend that his last words were "Doesn't anyone understand me?" No one was at his bedside when he died in the middle of the night January 12–13, 1941, after a stomach operation from which peritonitis resulted. "Is there one who understands me?" is what Anna Livia asks in the great final pages of *Finnegans Wake*, as the weary river winds safe to sea. She dies but will be reborn. Finn, again. We must reread the book until we understand it. If we do, we will understand the world.

Notes

[1] Stanislaus Joyce, *My Brother's Keeper* (1958), p. 109.

[2] Also a discontent with the idiotic simplicities of most political discourse, perhaps. In declining to comment on the Irish political scene for the *Journal de Genève* in 1916, Joyce noted that "the problem of my people is so complicated that one has need of all the resources of a plastic art to sketch it—without resolving it. I am of the opinion that no personal pronouncement is any longer permitted me." See Dominic Manganiello, *Joyce's Politics* (1981).

[3] See John Gatt-Rutter, *Italo Svevo: A Double Life* (1988).

[4] Sorel was the volatile French anarchist who began as a Marxist but under Vico's influence came to believe that revolutionary socialism should value the class struggle not as a means to some materialist utopia but as a way of reviving a degenerate culture through primitivism. Joyce's politics was vaguely anarchist; he admired not only Sorel but Max Stirner and a political writer of this same persuasion named Benjamin Tucker.

[5] Bernard Benstock, *Joyce-Again's Wake* (1965), p. 237.

[6] Joyce's great Irish friend and contemporary, the poet William Butler Yeats,

also was fond of a dualism of moon/night/softness/ideal world versus sun/day/ hard reality. In 1921, the year Joyce began *Finnegans Wake*, Bertrand Russell, seriously ill in China, became delirious and had a dream which he reported in a letter to Ottoline Morrell: "In the land of sleep there are rich visions . . . "; it is the opposite of the real world of "death & rivalry & effort."

[7] Cf. J. I. M. Stewart, *Eight Modern Writers* (1963).

[8] See P. N. Furbank, *Unholy Pleasure, or, The Idea of Social Class* (1985), pp. 134 ff.

[9] In 1902 August Strindberg, in "A Dream Play," tried to reproduce the disconnected and bizarre forms of a dream. One of its features is that "the characters split, double, multiply, they evaporate, crystallize, scatter and converge" (Graham Hough). The consciousness of the dreamer, which holds all this together, must in some sense be a universal, transpersonal phenomenon. The mildly manic Swedish genius Strindberg was probably a strong influence on *Finnegans Wake*.

SARTRE

From Joyce to Sartre, nearly a generation apart, the sense of alienation grew apace. By the time Jean-Paul Sartre came of age in the second decade of the twentieth century there existed what Richard Terdiman has called "a hundred-year-old tradition of attempts to understand why living has become unlivable." The first "unhappy consciousness," as Hegel termed it, belonged to the Romantics of the period from about 1780 to 1820. Amid a world now committed to inconstancy and change they yearned for the innocence of an imagined lost utopia ("How much better it would have been to have been born in 1600," Stendhal sighed). Youngsters in the 1830s burnt the flag, let their hair grow long, took drugs—those who did this 130 years later did not know they were echoing such even then antique gestures. Sensitive individuals unable to find peace amid the "sick hurry and divided aims" of modern life wearied of Romantic nostalgia and turned next, in terms of artistic style, to stern and grim Realism, with which they exposed the horrors of "bourgeois" society. They hated this society so much that they fantasized, with Flaubert, of burning its great cities down. As a strategy of coming to terms with a world that mocked their dreams and ideals, they withdrew into pure literature—or perhaps pure science.

The term "intellectual," it has been alleged, came into currency only toward the end of the nineteenth century.[1] Like most such terms (Wittgenstein would have been delighted to explain) this one is vague and

85

variously used. Sometimes it denoted those "accursed poets" and "bo-hemian" artists who flung deviant defiance at the mainstream society from cafés and attics around the turn of the century. But it might mean the scientific intellectual, a rather new type that comes to the fore in the later nineteenth century—a century that saw the unprecedented organization and professionalization of the sciences and medicine. Most notably, there were those "men of letters" who were not academic mandarins but closer to Grub Street in their origins, who might write fiction but also wrote criticism, commentary, theory—people like Karl Marx and H. G. Wells, Bernard Shaw and Anatole France, August Strindberg and Leo Tolstoy.

Of all the forces assisting the rise into prominence of such types, the most important was probably the secularization of modern life. "A happy vicar I might have been two hundred years ago," George Orwell remarked in the 1940s. Functions once performed by clerics now fell to writers. The writer, at any rate, became almost the nineteenth cen-tury hero. How exciting to emerge from poverty and obscurity to be idolized by millions, solely because of books—slender, dangerous pack-ages of social dynamite, containing messages of salvation, novels with characters more real than actual people because one could know them better and feel them more intensely. The old gospels and saints could not compete with the Sands, Dickenses, Balzacs, Flauberts, Hardys, and Zolas who now set souls and minds on fire. They were the new evangelists and superheroes. Paradoxically, this was partly because they were outcasts detested by "respectable" people. They were also very attractive to the opposite sex: "The artist," Sigmund Freud observed, "has won through his fantasy what before he could win only *in* his fantasy: honor, power, and the love of women."

Jean-Paul Sartre grew up surrounded by these books which in his grandfather's well-stocked library took on an aura of mystery and ex-citement. He described this in his autobiography of early childhood, titled *Les Mots*—the Words. An obsession with one of those books, *Madame Bovary*, haunted him all his life, as he indulged in a love-hate relationship with Flaubert, the archetypal alienated artist-intellectual. It was a role Sartre long sought to avoid, and yet he himself, an odd and awkward child, became this type *par excellence*. Of all our group he is the most typical "man of letters." Joyce, scarcely comfortable in this role, did not cultivate a literary personality. Sartre was far more versatile than any of our others. Novelist, playwright, philosopher, political and social theorist, and psychologist, he also became activist and important public personage. Called "the Voltaire of the modern age," he led an extremely active personal life. Alone of our group, indeed, he had a number of mistresses and innumerable sexual adventures. None of the others had anything approaching an adventurous private life; they all sublimated such desires completely. Of course, Sartre is our only Frenchman.

Literature, according to a Freudian interpretation, springs from the disappointed child inventing a new father. Sartre was the most father-less of our five specimens, though all the others save Wittgenstein had more or less disappointing fathers (and Ludwig's may have been too overpowering). Sartre wrote that "if my father had lived, I would know my rights and duties; he died [when Jean-Paul was two] and I do not know them." With his rather immature mother, the child went to live with his grandfather, an imposing, stuffy man who treated his daughter like a child and practiced a forbidding Calvinist religion (though he also led a rather vigorous sexual life). Sartre's hatred of religion, re-spectability, the "bourgeois" virtues may have sprung from his clashes with his grandfather, who subsequently opposed Sartre's choice of a literary career. Still, there is no doubt that Professor Charles Schweitzer, a relative of the famous Alsatian doctor Albert Schweitzer, loved and was kind to his grandson, while Sartre's feelings were more ambivalent than he later liked to pretend. He was in fact quite a petted and spoiled child.

Sartre's memorable self-portrait of his childhood, written many years later, is far from flattering, yet ultimately somewhat self-pitying: these adults manipulated him, forced him into desperate attempts to please them, created yet frustrated his identity. He escaped into the world of books. He wanted to be a writer, and found his identity, his self-image in this role. "By writing I was existing, I was escaping from the grown-ups." Like most children of his time (he was born in 1905) he also encountered the new art form, the cinema. He enjoyed reading comic books. And the hero of Sartre's first and most famous novel, Roquen-tin, finds some consolation in a popular song on a phonograph record. Sartre was a child of the twentieth-century media revolution much more than the others we have treated. Freud appeared in a film about himself, Joyce was fascinated by radio and television, as *Finnegans Wake* readers know, and Wittgenstein unwound by gaping at grade B movies, but Sartre's world was, much more than theirs, saturated with the ur-

ban culture of our times, a swirl of shapes and sounds far different from
the old bookish one.

It was a great shock to Jean-Paul when his mother remarried in 1917.
They went to live in La Rochelle, where he attended the local *lycée* for
three years before returning to Paris in 1920 to go to school. Somewhat
wild and undisciplined, Sartre the schoolboy nevertheless worked hard
and developed keen intellectual interests, with special debts to
Nietzsche and Dostoyevsky. He and his boyhood friend Paul Nizan
gained admission to the Ecole Normale Supérieure, where the top students in all France gathered. Sartre described his years there between
1924 and 1929 as happy ones, but he did not find what he wanted in
the professors, supposedly the best in France. An important influence
on both Sartre and Simone de Beauvoir (and also Simone Weil) was his
teacher at the *lycée* which prepared students for the Ecole, the writer
who called himself Alain (Emile Chartier). Like Alain's, Sartre's interest
was in literature and philosophy. He had the rare ability to fuse these
two domains; more specifically, to write novels and plays in which serious ideas come vividly to life, not just as sermons, but embodied
in the very lives of people. Only Dostoyevsky, perhaps, ever did this
better.

Sartre studied philosophy seriously, but he also turned to the great
French prose stylists. Marcel Proust and André Gide, the scintillating
contemporary novelists, were his special favorites. And though Sartre
occasionally deplored his inability to write poetry, Baudelaire and Mallarmé also deeply affected him. The literary life, the writer as hero or
magician, fascinated him. Sartre was a child of the modernist revolution
in literature as much as he was of the new philosophy. He put the two
together in an exciting way. Between 1931 and 1939, as he taught at a
series of schools, he continued to read, write, and on vacations travel
with the special friend he had meet at the Ecole, the brilliant and attractive Simone de Beauvoir.

Sartre belonged to the generation that just missed the Great War and
that came of age during the depressed and insecure, though intellectually and esthetically exciting years between the world wars. It was a
generation uniquely estranged from its predecessor. Evelyn Waugh
thought it the first time in English history there had been a serious gap
between old and young. A new moral world seemed to have dawned,
as the "acids of modernity" eroded ancestral values and the Russian
Revolution challenged their very foundations. Freud and Einstein were

part of it; but for Sartre the most challenging and subversive ideas came from the new currents in philosophy represented by phenomenology and existentialism. The source of the former was Edmund Husserl, a contemporary of Freud's whose pioneer work appeared in 1900. A much more accessible, even prophetic figure was Husserl's student Martin Heidegger whose *Sein und Zeit* (Being and Time) created in 1927 a sensation in intellectual circles. From these German sources (Husserl like Freud was Austro-Jewish, but taught at Freiburg in Germany most of his career) Sartre drew the essential elements of his thought, though he put his own distinctive stamp on them. During 1933–34, on the advice of Raymond Aron, he went to Germany to study these German thinkers.

The idea behind Sartre's first, sensationally successful novel *Nausea*, which he wrote in his early thirties, was a Husserlian one. The founder of phenomenology had proposed to get at the "consciousness" that underlies all knowledge,[2] discovering its *a priori* or given structure by "bracketing" all content; suspending as it were everything that comes into consciousness in order to find out what it is like in itself. (A comparison might be taking all the merchandise off a store's shelves to find the shape and arrangement of those shelves.) Sartre transforms this idea into a young man who finds himself lost in a gloomy provincial city without friends, job, permanent residence, any but the barest possessions. A student, Roquentin's only function is working on a dissertation in which he ceases to believe. The facts of history, he decides, are irrational and absurd; imposing some system on them to make them seem rational is dishonest. Roquentin has been stripped of all roles, down to the hard core of his bare humanity.

In this state of pure freedom, released from being determined by others, Roquentin first experiences nausea—at his own face in the mirror, his flesh, his "facticity"—and a schizoid sense of his outer self being an inert object. (Compare Albert Camus's *Stranger*.) He recovers, at least partially, by realizing that he is absolutely free to make himself. His inner being is radically different from other kinds of being. As Sartre will explain in his philosophical work *Being and Nothingness*, published five years later in 1943, consciousness is not bound by any laws such as those that determine physical matter; it is in fact a kind of nothingness, a pure receptivity, "a hole in being" that does not exist unless it responds to something external. Of course, it may create some object in the mind, an idea, for example, of the self. Unlike Husserl,

Sartre did not see consciousness as having any essence, any determinate structure. It is pure protean negativity; but for that very reason it is infinitely free and can choose anything it likes to fashion its own being. There is no self, but consciousness can manufacture one, any one it wants. All this had the ring of truth (what *is* our consciousness, we might ask ourselves? Can we conceptualize it? It slips away from us and cannot be made into an object). And Roquentin was a most appropriate metaphysical hero for our time, when the plight of man is indeed so often loneliness, anomie, uncertain identity. The existentialists had a remedy: face the awful but bracing truth that we can choose, act, and make ourselves whatever we will. Their ethical injunction was total sincerity, "authenticity": do not let others determine your being.

Nevertheless we cannot do without other people; without them we are that vague nothingness that is (in Sartre's vocabulary, taken from Hegel) being-for-itself. Remember that consciousness must have objects; likewise if it is to have any solid sort of being it needs others to constitute it. Being constituted by others is humiliating, but a person can hardly do without it. So the plight of humanity is irremediable, the young Sartre seemed to say. Man is "a useless passion." His nature is to be that which he is not and not to be that which he is. Insofar as he has a secure identity he must live in bad faith, the slave of others. If he lives authentically he will suffer from isolation and anxiety. Your choice of poisons, as a poet put it. Love is the worst—that game of mirrors lovers play, each trying vainly to capture the other's pure subjectivity, trying to avoid being objectified, destined to end in frustration. In Sartre's famous play *No Exit* (1944), "hell is other people" whom we can neither live with nor without.

Sartre meanwhile had become, surprisingly, something of a national hero. The war had brought the subjection of France to the Nazis or to those Frenchmen who abjectly carried out their orders. The situation that faced any French person, whether to submit and collaborate with the German rulers or join the underground movement of resistance, illustrated Sartre's point that we must choose. The war changed him. In his youth a pure intellectual, thinking only of his writing, he now became an activist. "The war taught me that one must be engaged, committed." A prisoner of war for nearly a year after the fall of France in June 1940, Sartre found solidarity with people of all sorts in the prison camp. "Never were we so free as when enslaved." (Unlike Mathieu, in Sartre's autobiographical novel *Death in the Soul*, Sartre did not die defiantly fighting the Germans but was quietly captured after all his officers had surrendered.) He wrote a play for the people of Stalag XII, a parable on the theme of resisting oppression. Then after contriving his release from the camp he played some part in the resistance. His play *The Flies* (*Les Mouches*) performed in Paris in 1943 brought him prominently to public attention. The German authorities who allowed its production evidently failed to see the message that lay beneath the surface of the classical Greek tragedy about Orestes, who slays a tyrant as he avenges his father's death at the hands of his mother and her lover.

Needless to say Sartre's Orestes is given a new twist; he is an existentialist hero who, refusing to believe in the gods, turns the Furies into the harmless eponymous flies. Sartre's talent for making absorbing drama out of ideas continued in *No Exit* (*Huis Clos*), probably his best known play, which was performed in Paris during the liberation of 1944. At this same time *Being and Nothingness* established his reputation as a pure philosopher. This exciting debut of a versatile talent paralleled the dramatic history of France in World War II—the shocking defeat, the crisis of conscience, the final victory. Sartre and France came together in a remarkable way to create one of the great intellectual stories of this century.

During the exciting scenes accompanying the liberation of Paris, as American troops forbore to enter the city until the French had a chance to help discomfit the retreating Germans, Sartre, writing in his friend Camus's paper *Combat*, exhorted Parisians to "hit a German over the head and take his revolver . . . get hold of a car, with the car take an armoured car and a tank." It is doubtful if many French people took Sartre's advice; certainly he himself hit no Germans over the head, though he and Simone narrowly escaped when a bomb hit their train. A fiesta atmosphere surrounded the events of August 1944. Some have argued that only a small percentage of the French participated in the existentialist drama of resistance versus collaboration; for most, life went on rather as usual. That Simone went skiing not long before the liberation suggests a certain business- (or pleasure-) as-usual aspect of life, more so than one might have imagined.

Sartre's reputation spread far beyond France. As his plays and books appeared in other countries, a war-shocked world made existentialism a buzzword, Sartre and Camus its prophets. The message was the timely one: that against all odds we may by courageous thought and action snatch salvation from total despair. Wary pessimism about all panaceas accompanied the lesson that humanity might restore itself to a semblance of sanity by looking at real human beings rather than abstractions. It was just the right mixture of pessimism and optimism. Those who accused existentialism of gloomy nihilism were no more right than those who saw in it an almost Polyannish hopefulness. After the Nazis, the Holocaust, the war's barbaric destruction on both sides it would have been almost obscene to repeat nineteenth-century hymns to progress. The troubles of our proud and angry dust are from eternity and will not fail. But evil can at least by minimized by integrity, sincerity, and respect for the existent person. There is a far side of despair that is disabused hope. In any case nothing is determined, and human beings have total freedom to choose their values and act on them. Even in a Nazi concentration camp or a Stalinist prison, under duress or torture, a person can refuse and negate this evil.

More than a few noticed the chameleon-like quality of the existentialist ethic, which asked only total sincerity in making a choice based on one's particular situation. To those who applied to him for advice Sartre was inclined to say, make up your own mind, just be sure you are totally sincere and do not lean on rules made by others. Politically, the result might be a quasi-conservatism, hostile to all ideologies, those "smelly little orthodoxies" (as George Orwell called them), including Communism as well as Nazism, that had poisoned the interwar years. Sartre felt this way for a time after the war. He had never shown much interest in Marxism, and his writings during 1945–47 dismiss official Marxism as a debased philosophy with harmful effects ("the policy of Stalinist Communism is incompatible with the honest exercise of the literary profession.") He associated himself with an anti-Stalinist "Socialism and Liberty" group. He founded a brief-lived Rally for Revolutionary Democracy which included some ex-Trotskyites, and he supported Yugoslavia's dissident Communists in their tilts with Stalin. The Communist party denounced him. His popular play *Dirty Hands* (*Les mains sales*), which he later tried to suppress, seemed to rebuke the bad faith of those who surrender their will to the party. His friend and fellow existentialist Albert Camus, like George Orwell in England, became almost obsessively convinced that the "concentration camp socialism" into which Russian Communism had degenerated was a monstrous fraud from which true socialism needed to be rescued. Sartre himself was not far from this position between about 1946 and

1950, the years of the democratic rally against the USSR which gave rise to the Marshall Plan and NATO alliance.

On the other hand the Communist party was strong in postwar France; it had earned credits by valiant service in the wartime resistance. Sartre had met and learned to respect Communists in the Underground. He wished not so much to oppose Communism as to rescue it from the dead hand of Stalinism, which he saw as intellectually bankrupt and morally debased. Its mechanical materialism actually destroyed the possibility of revolution, since it neglected the all-important subjective side; robots do not rebel, for the decision to rebel takes place in a consciousness. Sartre presented himself as a better Communist than the Soviet rulers—more royalist than the king! His offer to help them out by supplying a more up-to-date philosophy and psychology naturally did not please the Kremlin priests. This bohemian with his pessimistic subjectivism and his ties to Heidegger impressed them as even sinister. French Communist intellectuals who later apologized to him called him a fascist at this time. But Sartre's popularity with young French radicals could hardly be dismissed. In these years as editor of *Les temps modernes* (he took the title from Charlie Chaplin's film) Sartre was at the center of the most exciting ideas of his time.

Raymond Aron told Sartre he could not be the heir of both Marx and Kierkegaard, but Jean-Paul thought he could. Marx was changed out of all recognition when the Critical Theorists of the Frankfurt School, and others, examined a body of his heretofore unpublished and largely unknown writings. These scholars charged the Soviets with using his writings selectively and suppressing much, offering only one reading where other, quite different ones were possible. Sartre found this "new" Marx, rescued from the Kremlin bureaucrats, quite exciting; not surprisingly, Marx turns out to look like an existentialist who declares that men and women make their own history by their free choices. Their subjectivity interacts with an ossified social order that is the product of past struggles with a niggardly nature. In choosing to revolt they overcome alienation and forge real bonds of interpersonal communication.

Sartre came to believe that Marxism, of this existentialized sort, is the necessary, basic philosophy for modern man: "our thoughts, whatever they are, can take shape only upon this humus." The assertion struck many as bizarre. By 1951 Sartre had evidently passed over to orthodox Communism; though he never joined it, he was saying that one must not criticize the Communist party even if it was wrong, that the USSR was a free society, or even—if we read his play *The Devil and the Good Lord* this way—that ruthless tyrants were necessary. He broke with Camus and Merleau-Ponty, the other leading French existentialists, because of what they saw as his ultra-bolshevism, inconsistent with existentialist belief in freedom. The Cold War pulled Sartre away from the Americans, whom he accused of practicing germ warfare in the Korean War of 1950–53. (Whether in fact the Pentagon did at least consider such a weapon remains a matter of some controversy.) In 1954 he was an honored guest in the USSR, drinking so much vodka he had to be hospitalized upon his return.

One can perhaps explain Sartre's pro-Communist stance by his commitment to commitment, his belief that one must always choose a side. The world did indeed seemed to be forced to choose between Russia and the United States in the early 1950s, and Sartre made his choice. The worst about Stalin's mass murders was just being revealed; the French Communist party refused to believe it as late as 1950 when two famous lawsuits publicized the issue. Certainly, as Simone de Beauvoir's interesting memoirs make clear, Sartre's circle was earnestly debating this in 1950. Stalin died in 1953, but not until 1956 did the new party leaders concede some of his crimes. Khrushchev's sensational "secret speech" to the party congress of that year sent shock waves through the party and the world, and for many people this was the first revelation that the great socialist experiment was based on the death and suffering of millions. Heretofore these atrocities had been suppressed by the sympathy of the world's intellectuals for the Russian Revolution, with its goal of transforming mankind, and then by Russia's heroic struggle against Nazi Germany in World War II.

Sartre's pro-Soviet phase, an embarrassment to his reputation, was interrupted in 1956 when Russian suppression of Hungary's bid for a freer Communism brought mass resignations from the party in France. Sartre was deeply shocked and never again quite trusted the party. After 1956 he withdrew to write his own treatise of social theory, another massive tome on the order of *Being and Nothingness*, this one called *Critique of Dialectical Reason*. Sartre believed "we must show the world that true Marxism is not Stalinism." Like Marx, Sartre never finished his sociological synthesis, nor is the one completed volume entirely successful. His constant companion Beauvoir pictured him laboring at it through sleepless nights of coffee and pills. It contains some striking metaphors, none at bottom too original, on the themes of alienation and revolution. According to critics its task was an inherently impossible one, that of imposing a system on the existentialist world of free human choices, and the contradictions show. The unfinished second volume includes a segment published separately as *The Ghost of Stalin*, in which Sartre exorcised his past by perceptively analyzing what went wrong with the Russian Revolution.

He did not cease to believe in revolution. The *Critique* expands on the idea that a true revolution can bring people together in a spontaneously created community. The barriers between them are overcome and they cease to be "serialized," i.e. associated only in artificial, mechanical, bureaucratic ways, like people waiting for a bus. The Hungarian revolution of 1956, which the Russians suppressed, was such a happening. Sartre also militantly defended the Algerian revolt which shook France in the mid–1950s. What may be his best play, *The Condemned of Altona* (as *Les séquestrés d'Altona* is usually translated) was perceived as a commentary on French barbarities in Algeria, though nominally the play is about a German Nazi torturer who has survived in isolation to the present, i.e., 1959. In 1960, after pro-Algerian independence demonstrations, angry French Algerians bombed Sartre's apartment. The deeply divisive question was resolved in favor of independence for Algeria only after General Charles de Gaulle, whom Sartre had bitterly opposed, became the leader of a new French regime.

Sartre maintained some contact with the Soviets during the Khrushchev years. He refused to join the protests on behalf of Boris Pasternak when Khrushchev (in what he subsequently recognized as a mistake) persecuted the great Russian writer for publishing *Dr. Zhivago* in the West. In 1963 Sartre and Beauvoir visited Moscow in connection with plans for an East-West writers' organization for the exchange of ideas, but found Khrushchev surly. The Khrushchev "thaw" had recongealed, and the Soviet leader now agreed with Maurice Thorez, the French Communist leader, that Sartre was a dangerous reactionary. Jean-Paul, in Prague later that year for a writers' conference, responded that to brand Freud, Kafka, and Joyce as "decadent," the official Soviet line, was to preclude a dialogue.

The dismal Brezhnev years that followed Khrushchev's fall in 1964 ended the last of Sartre's illusions about Soviet-style Communism. Russian intervention to crush Czechoslovakia's "socialism with a human face" in 1968 was the last straw. By that time, Sartre was absorbed in the New Left and about to emerge as prophet of the memorable student revolution of May 1968.

He addressed 10,000 students at the peak of this experiment in utopian politics. Of the student uprisings all over the world in the mid to late 1960s, Sartre was not the only inspiration; perhaps Mao Zedong's Chinese Communism was the foremost, and there were all the other maverick Marxists—namely Lukacs, Gramsci, and others.[3] But more than any other one person he symbolized its spirit and articulated its ideals. Unfortunately this rare moment when *pour-soi* (being-for-itself) and *en-soi* (being-in-itself) fused did not last. Sartre turned to the Maoists, but in the end the Chinese failed him too.

Many found Sartre politically outrageous in his later years. He joined with Bertrand Russell in trying to put the United States on trial for war crimes in Vietnam; he defended the Baader-Meinhof gang of German terrorists. Hysterically anti-American during the Vietnam War, he once requested the Russians to use nuclear weapons against the Americans.[4] But he was not as one-sided as some would have it. He and Simone protested Castro's arrest of the poet Padilla, as well as Soviet violations of human rights (the arrest of Sakharov, for example). He criticized the Syrian government as well as the Israeli. It is perhaps not well known that in his last year he approved of the boycott of the Olympic Games in Moscow, sponsored by American President Carter in response to the Soviet invasion of Afghanistan; and he rallied to the cause of the Vietnamese "boat people" fleeing from the government Sartre had once so enthusiastically supported. Sartre's right to be called the "conscience of the world" can be defended (as can Bertrand Russell's, the other self-appointed supervisor of world political morals). He fairly consistently opposed what he saw as assaults on human liberty from whatever political direction they came, except perhaps between 1950 and 1956 when he was uncritically pro-Soviet. Initially he was not very concerned with women's rights, but later he grew more sympathetic to Simone de Beauvoir's feminist perspective.

He did grow rather more disillusioned. "No political party offers any hope at all." "I cannot see how it is possible to resolve the problems which are brought about by any institutionalized structure." He no longer called himself a Marxist. So much for the whole *Critique* enterprise, which he abandoned. Back to literature! Back, in fact, to the book that had fascinated him as a child: he spent most of his later intellectual energies on an enormous psychobiography of Gustave Flaubert, leading up to the moment *Madame Bovary* was conceived. It could be said that Flaubert was really Jean-Paul Sartre, the alienated bourgeois writer; Joyce's Stephen Dedalus or Shem. Struggle as he might, Sartre could not escape his role as a bourgeois intellectual, a mere writer.

In his last years, Sartre continued to devote much of his enormous energy to amorous adventures. Neurotic intellectual or conscience of the world, the modern Voltaire or a parlor pink, he had become more widely famous than any serious writer of his time. His funeral procession in 1980 drew a huge crowd, almost rivalling those of de Gaulle's, Kennedy's, and Churchill's in this age of the mammoth public funeral.

It might be best to draw a discreet curtain around Sartre's attempts at world-saving. It is his existentialist psychology that counts. Existentialism was one of the greatest "happenings" in the history of ideas, for when it flashed across the postwar scene it captivated a generation, less by its vision of a proud, world-making freedom than by its striking dissection of subjective and inter-subjective reality. No other psychology had such a ring of truth. Surely this was because it related so closely to people's experience in our age. The problematic of existentialist psychology is the precarious, doubly threatened self. It is threatened by objectification, which is implict in the very nature of being. To the subjective consciousness of others I must appear as an object, for subjective consciousness can only know objects. It must constitute me as a role, a type; I am a professor or a comedian or a waiter, expected to play whatever part I am assigned. I rely on this for my identity; it is all that I have save that dizzying indeterminacy which is my own consciousness, and which in turn makes objects of others. "I am seen, therefore I am" was this modern Descartes' summation.

This other-constituted self gives rise to deep anxieties, for I know it is not the real me, and I resent being made an object of; I am dependent on others for my being, and they may withdraw it at any time. (I may think the class sees me as a brilliant and profound professor, but they may suddenly decide that I am just a pompous ass, and I am deflated.) The gaze of the other humiliates me as it converts me into an object; I am constituted and I cannot control this. My only recourse is to do the same to him or her.

Losing confidence in this unsatisfactory role-playing object as a self, which is a fabrication, I may "detach an inner or ghostly self, a transcendent ego never to be tested by confrontation with others. So a chain reaction of disintegration of the ego can begin" (Stuart Hampshire). The existentialist analysis of schizophrenia is a compelling one. As with Freud, this insanity is seen not as a freakish disease but as something implicit in the human situation; it is hardly too much to say that we all by virtue of being human beings tremble on the edge of madness.

Existential psychiatrists like R. D. Laing experience all kinds of difficulty with the doctor-patient roles, which they see as inherently false. They do not want to reduce the mental state to anything else, to "interpret" it, as other psychoanalysts tend to do, but to take it on its own terms and try to enter into the lived world of the person regarded as crazy or experiencing personality problems, and see things as he or she does. The affinities with Wittgensteinian therapy are evident. The editors of *Les temps modernes* once heatedly debated an article Sartre insisted on having published in which a defiant patient assailed his psychoanalyst for never looking him in the face. Laing reflected Sartre's views in rejecting the bad faith of the doctor-patient relationship and asking for simply a human one.[5]

The existentialist analysis seems especially relevant in the present era, subject as it is to a built-in schizoid effect: the "double bind" of, on the one hand, an enriched consciousness, fed by education, literacy, and the audio-visual media; and on the other an ant-like economic society that demands highly specialized, often deadly boring functions. Withal, a culturally chaotic world where scores of different value systems and languages demand that the personality whirl about in a sea of change.

A newspaper story tells of a man who suddenly exploded into a terrible crime, murdering his wife and children or his employer perhaps; interviews with those who knew him stress how unbelievable this was because he was such a "normal person," so quiet and well-behaved, so disciplined and orderly. But the inner fantasy life flourished precisely because the outer self was detached from it, playing its social roles like an automaton. The seething volcano within finally crashed through the robot on the outside.

Existential and phenomenological psychiatry received influences from the philosophers Martin Heidegger, who gave seminars at the Zurich clinic; and Karl Jaspers, who began as an M.D., turned then to psychiatry and finally to philosophy. (Compare the paths of Wittgenstein and Musil.) Sartre wrote quite a few psychobiographical studies; in addition to the work on Flaubert and his autobiographical *The*

Words, he analyzed the poet Baudelaire, Kaiser Wilhelm II, and the anti-Semitic personality. Indeed, all his stories, plays, and novels are basically psychobiographical or psychohistorical; in a few cases it is hard to say whether we have a story or a treatise. He wrote the screen play for John Huston's movie about Sigmund Freud, though his original script turned out to be impractically long. So Sartre made a distinctive contribution to perhaps the most promising area of psychiatry. He described himself as a "critical fellow-traveller" of psychoanalysis.

It is an open question whether in the end his psychology will not prove to be his greatest contribution, outlasting the sociology of *Critique of Dialectical Reason* and the pure philosophy of *Being and Nothingness* (though this is hard to separate from the psychology); outliving his literary works considered strictly as art. His plays, even *No Exit*, do not seem to be performed much any more. The novels are interesting for what they tell us about Sartre, not as works of literature per se. (In her acute study of the novels, Iris Murdoch noticed that their characters suffer from being analyzed too much.) It is his life itself, as a work of art or an amazing twentieth-century phenomenon, that we must place first. None of our other figures lived anywhere near so extensively and vigorously. Sartre, the prophet of the lonely self, the archetype of the alienated intellectual, was oddly enough a man of immense social activity. As editor, debater, lecturer, polemicist, he was at the center for three decades not only of French intellectual life, but often of its political life. In 1960 thousands of veterans marched through Paris streets shouting "Kill Sartre!" In 1968 10,000 students overflowed a theater to hear him tell them why they were rebelling. When in 1970 President de Gaulle, remarking that "you don't arrest Voltaire," refused to have the philosopher detained for selling illegal Maoist pamplets, the world was fascinated by this encounter.

He became the friend and consultant of leading world political leaders. An inveterate traveller ever since the early days when he and Simone tramped over Africa and Greece, sometimes sleeping under the stars, Sartre later visited China, Cuba, Brazil, the United States, the Soviet Union, and many other countries. Then there were his numerous love affairs, which occasionally strained but never really threatened his enduring relationship with Simone de Beauvoir. The writer who so memorably diagnosed the frustrations of sexual love never tired of testing his theories in practice.

Mme. de Beauvoir was a notable figure in her own right. A fellow

Normalien with Sartre, she ranked second from the top of the list of qualifiers for the class of 1928 (behind another woman, the remarkable Simone Weil), becoming one of the first four or five women to enter the famous Ecole after it was opened to women in 1924. She was nearly Sartre's intellectual equal and a vital contributor to his ideas, which some think should be considered their joint production. Her own book *The Second Sex* ranks as a leading contribution to modern feminism. It was existential in the sense of showing the life-meaning of being a woman, the ways in which, for example, girls saw their future differently from boys and had their choices restricted. Later she discussed with equal vividness the realities of aging *(La Vieillesse)*: the way society dictates roles for the elderly which contrast sharply with their inner feelings. A prolific writer, she poured forth in novels and autobiographical works scenes from their richly peopled life more extensively than Jean-Paul. An early novel was based on the *ménage à trois* which Sartre imposed during his love affair with a Russian girl. In *The Mandarins*, Camus, Aron, Mauriac, and the whole glittering cast of postwar French intellectual life as well as their earnest debates about politics and life are displayed. She had little novelistic imagination; the writing was always about her own experiences, whether disguised as fiction or called autobiography. And it is quite uncritical; its worst feature is an overpowering self-righteousness that admits no other legitimate point of view than hers and Sartre's. But it is always alive and questing for reality.

Faced with the dismaying fact of interminable meetings, Simone was less enthusiastic about "commitment" than Jean-Paul or Simone Weil; in *The Second Sex* she declined to consider herself a "feminist." But in her later years she campaigned actively for women's rights. She did not allow Sartre's succesion of other mistresses (and a couple of aberrations of her own) to impair their close companionship. The most flagrant of these was Sartre's adoption of an Algerian Jewish girl, Arlette Elkaim, as his daughter, which it must be admitted was almost too much for Simone, since it resulted in Sartre's properties being handed over on his death to Arlette. Beauvoir riposted by herself adopting a daughter; and the years since Sartre's death have witnessed a tug of war over his literary remains (a vast quantity of letters and notebooks containing highly intimate material) between the heirs. In 1983 Beauvoir published a selection of Sartre's letters which, it is alleged, makes him look worse than he was.[6] This was perhaps evidence of a sense of betrayal. The adoption of Arlette was typically Sartrean in its deliberate flouting of respectable opinion. Sartre was a compulsive heretic, a hater of the bourgeoisie from which he sprang, which had treated him so well, and to which in some sense he always (to his chagrin) continued to belong. He found a reason to refuse the Nobel Prize when it was offered to him in 1964. (It was never offered to Freud or Joyce or Wittgenstein; of these only the last might have imitated Sartre's gesture of disdain for the bauble, probably from a somewhat different and worthier motive.[7]) Sartre's many campaigns on behalf of the oppressed suffer a little from the suspicion that he is just revenging himself on a society that once made him feel odd and unwanted. Something in his lonely childhood marked him for life with an obsessive nonconformism, a desire to stick out his tongue at stuffy citizens. His was the most neurotic personality of our quintet, more so even than Wittgenstein, or at least neurotic in a far more demonstrative way: mistresses, heavy smoking and liquor consumption, even mescaline and amphetamines[8]. One may suspect his anti-Establishment antics of being self-serving. There was something spurious—bad faith?—about the claims of Sartre and Beauvoir to represent "the people." The title of the Maoist newspaper Sartre joined as an editor in 1970 was *The Cause of the People*. He was too busy with his Flaubert biography to give it his full attention, but in a well-publicized incident he appeared in the street to sell it, thus challenging de Gaulle to martyrize him.

"Writing is an escape, a sign of weakness," he had said. It is, he agreed with Freud, a result of neurosis. Yet in the end Sartre accepted again that he was first and foremost a writer. But if Sartre was neurotic we may be glad of it, since it provided him with those marvelous psychological insights and the compulsion to write them down.

The extent, range, and generally high quality of Sartre's writings constitute an impressive achievement. When we add up his action-filled life we have indeed a modern Voltaire, another Balzac or Hugo, stamped with the twentieth century's peculiar neurasthenia. More than any of our other figures Sartre attempted to enter into the life of his era, sharing as much of its experiences as he could. He is the only one of them who seriously attempted to live as well as to think and write. "The intellect of man must choose," Yeats wrote, "perfection of the life or of the work." Accepting this as the fate of the modern, Joyce poured everything into his work. Wittgenstein was very nearly the pure thinker, uninterested in anything else. The underpinning of Freud's imposing intellectual life was a conventional, unadventurous private one, as was also the case with Einstein. They took some part in the affairs of their professional scientific organizations and dabbled feebly from time to time in politics, but one can find little integration of their lives with those of the vast majority of their fellow human beings, at least not in the personal, human, involved way that existentialism means.

One might object that we can say the same of Sartre: in most ways he was wildly untypical. More than any of the others, he hated, with a fierce and implacable hatred, what he called the bourgeoisie, meaning really the average person. Sartre seems to have had a weaker ego, a basic ontological insecurity of the sort he so brilliantly examined in his writings. His politics and his lifestyle were both aggressively aimed at scandalizing generally accepted social norms, to a degree far exceeding the other cases we have considered. Though Joyce and Wittgenstein distanced themselves from a society they scarcely felt comfortable with, neither spent much time attempting to affront it; they simply went their own ways. Joyce in the end came to terms with that ordinary human world in a way Sartre never did. It is significant that whereas Joyce eventually married Nora, Sartre never did legalize his relationship with Simone. He never had a child until he adopted his mistress near the end of his life. He travelled more than any of the others, and travel, "the yearning for new and distant scenes, craving for freedom, release, forgetfulness," a flight from one's own society, is a symptom of alienation. In this way Sartre resembled Thomas Mann's Leverkühn.

But Sartre lived more passionately and fully, in his world of fellow writers, artists, and actors perhaps because such a world had a greater vitality in France. It was a bohemian society, but an extensive and tolerated, even respected one. At the same time his political attempts to identify with the "people," flawed and even phony as these efforts might have been, were much more vigorous and fruitful than the others'— one thinks here of Einstein's naive lending of his name to various causes. Sartre lived in a whirl of activity, whether it was amorous or political (it was usually both at the same time). And he wrote down all of this. His letters to Simone, for example, describe in great detail his adventures with other women. *Les Mots*, the *Carnets* or notebooks (only some of which have been published as yet), and the long autobiographical series of novels called collectively "Roads to Liberty" (of which Sartre published three and wanted to finish three more) testify to this desire to record everything, to analyze each emotion and relationship. Each life situation was of absorbing interest to the existentialist. It had to be written about as well as lived. (Simone too, to the dismay of Nelson Allgren, wrote at great and intimate length in her published books about her love affair with him.)

Sartre shared with Joyce an interest in popular culture. He loved the Marx brothers and admired, though he clearly did not fully understand, aspects of American popular culture such as Tin Pan Alley songs and Keystone Cop movies—he identified this, curiously, with Jewish and black opposition to "bourgeois" American culture, thus managing to square his overall anti-Americanism with this taste for many American cultural products.

And Sartre's free-swinging life style, one may argue, has in fact increasingly become that of twentieth-century urban humanity. Traditional rules and constraints on personal life lost their authority. The so-called sexual revolution followed close on Sartre's emergence as culture hero. Freud, we recall, doubted that this would bring more happiness, and we may agree that it has not.[9] But it is irreversible nonetheless. So in this sense Sartre's *praxis* prefigured that of modern civilization in general. At one point he thought existentialism was only a method, and Marxism the essential content of present-day life. But he came to realize that existentialism is a separate philosophy or worldview. In fact it is the indispensable philosophy for modern man.

Notes

[1] T. W. Heyck finds the idea of "an intellectual life" emerging in the 1870s in Britain (*The Transformation of Intellectual Life in Victorian England*, 1982). The first recognition of the noun "intellectual" by the Oxford English Dictionary was in the 1888 edition (definition: "a person possessing or supposed to possess superior powers of intellect.") The origin of the term in France is often ascribed to the "Manifesto of the Intellectuals" published in early 1898 during the Dreyfus Affair.

[2] We might note a basic disagreement with Wittgenstein, for whom language precedes and determines thought (we cannot be said to have an idea unless we know words for it). To the phenomenologists something is already there in the human subject, which receives and shapes language.

[3] The beleaguered Russians, attempting in 1973 to cite all the misleaders and corrupters of youth, mentioned Scheler, Husserl, Unamuno, Heidegger, Jaspers, Camus, Garaudy, Adorno, Horkheimer, Marcuse, and Fromm. Promi-

nent in this list of course are existentialists and Frankfurt School neo-Marxists. Roger Garaudy was a defector from French Communism to left-wing Christianity.

[4] A curious parallel to Russell, that other modern Voltaire whom Sartre in some ways so much resembled (the versatility and charisma, the political involvement, the adventurous personal life), was that in their dotage both fell under the unfortunate influence of young radical doctrinaires who abused their power. In Sartre's case Benny Lévy would manipulate the philosopher in the same way that American Ralph Schoenman did Russell.

[5] Among Freud's disciples Sandor Ferenczi went a similar route; the analyst should be "only a human being with feelings," should "love" the patient and even let the patient analyze the doctor. For this he incurred the displeasure of Freud and ostracism by the psychoanalytical establishment. See his *Clinical Diary*, ed. Judith Dupont (1989).

[6] See M. Contat in *Le Monde*, 22 Sept. 1989.

[7] Sartre defended his action partly on the grounds that the Nobel was a capitalist prize, offered only to Western writers or to Soviet dissidents like Pasternak. He claimed that it should have been offered to Sholokhov, who was a better writer than Pasternak. André Breton called Sartre's action "a propaganda operation in support of the Eastern bloc" and "a perfectly gauged political action."

[8] Reviewing Mme. de Beauvoir's picture of the last years in her *Le cérémonie des adieux*, published after Sartre's death, John Weightman (*TLS*, Dec. 25, 1981) remarked that it shows Sartre "leading the existence of a dilettante, bourgeois intellectual." Perhaps enviously, Georges Bataille thought Sartre "of all bourgeois literary parasites, the slickest I know."

[9] See for example Celia Haddon, *The Limits of Sex* (1983).

Conclusion

LIKE all the truly great ones, our five giants were inimitable. No one like them has since appeared. They had no "disciples," not even Freud, whose followers became so fragmented that there virtually ceased to be *a* Freudian school. Novels might reverberate with echoes of Joyce but no one tried to write another *Finnegans Wake*; there was even a revolt against such pretentious myth-making in favor of much more direct and low-key fiction. Wittgenstein's remarks still fertilize philosophy, and very likely always will, but the *Tractatus* stands as a lonely, unique curiosity in the history of thought. And existentialism just about came to an end, as a movement, with Sartre. We retain its insights, but people do not often call themselves existentialists any more. So, too, compared to the crowd of highly proficient professionals who compete for grants and honors in the glamorous domain of nuclear physics, astrophysics, laser technology, etc., Einstein seems almost a quaint, old-fashioned figure.

If the works themselves were inimitable and unrepeatable, the "influences" of course continue, and so does the interest. There was a French-led Freud revival in the 1960s, and interest in him continues unabated to the present, to judge by the vital presence of his ideas in such areas as literature and biography. What is written in the name of psycho-analysis by academic critics today would undoubtedly have amazed Freud, as it amazes almost everyone outside this coterie. But it invokes his authority. Something similar is the case in physics, which honors

Einstein as a founding father while going far beyond him. In all the cases, we see what is after all a normal pattern of both absorbing and forgetting the contributions of past genius: these pass silently into the heritage while the books themselves are relegated to the shelf reserved for classics. Historians write scholarly articles about them.

Other important schools of thought and modes of writing appeared. A full account of the century's mind would have to make room for structuralism and deconstruction. The latter school owed something to both Wittgenstein and Sartre, as well as to their common mentor (and Freud's), Friedrich Nietzsche.[1] And Joyce: "everytime I write," said Derrida, "Joyce's ghost is always coming on board." The splitting and amalgamating of individual characters in *Finnegans Wake* foreshadows structuralist and poststructuralist elimination of personal identity in favor of linguistic discourses. One might argue that deconstruction was Wittgenstein crossed with Freud and Sartre; but in fact an even more important ingredient was structural linguistics and semiotics, or semiology, a strain with rather different roots.

This more recent intellectual activity has become excessively subtle and difficult. Relativity, the *Tractatus*, *Being and Nothingness*, *Finnegans Wake* were all bywords in their time for the hard to understand, but it is no exaggeration to say they are clarity itself compared with some of the exercises of Jacques Derrida, Jacques Lacan, Michel Foucault and other high priests of the new literary criticism—not to speak of their American followers. Those who practice this arcane art are a small handful of specialists. Einstein, Freud, Sartre, even Joyce and Wittgenstein kept at least a fragile connection to the general reader—reaching not everybody, to be sure, but a fair number of cultivated citizens who were not professional academics. Their names were known everywhere, even by the least educated. And at least a modicum of their thought passed into the popular, general culture. Almost nothing of that link now remains. The thought that passes muster with the various specialist communities in physics, philosophy, and literature is incomprehensible to 99 percent of those outside those charmed circles; it is even incomprehensible to specialists in other academic disciplines, or other coteries in the same one. There are different bands of literary critics who do not understand each others' jargon. The man in the street, though more highly educated today than formerly, does not know any serious thinker as his precursors knew Freud and Einstein, or even Joyce and Sartre (who were after all world famous). The best thought and literature has passed beyond the ken of the cultivated general public into the hands of specialists.

This was arguably the chief significance of our group: they represented a last stand of cultural unity against the forces of disintegration. These first-generation modernists were aware that only chaos could follow them—"after us the savage god," Yeats wrote. To most of their contemporaries they seemed to be that chaos. Compared to the nineteenth century's magnificent simplicities they were overly subtle, overly obscure, overly subjective. One can interpret their work as bringing the great tradition to an end and enthroning chaos. But compared to what came later they in fact achieved a rare balance between depth and breadth. Certainly they had not given up, as later would be the case, on the possibility of some overarching synthesis of knowledge, some mastery of the realm of the knowable. That, after all, is why Joyce created his monstrous book: he wanted to put the whole world into it. Sartre tried for something like a total synthesis of social, psychological, and historical reality. Wittgenstein may have given up on a system, but he cast the luminous light of his intelligence on a great number of areas, as he scorned the professional philosophers assembling in meetings to read technical papers. Einstein's pursuit of a single harmonious order beneath the apparent chaos of the new physics we know well; it is what increasingly estranged him from the bulk of his colleagues.

So these were the last to make the attempt at mastering the whole intellectul heritage and expressing it in works of art—the last sages. The postmodern deconstructivists have ridiculed this quest for certainty and totality, declaring themselves more than content (they protest too much) with pluralism, relativism, inconsistency. One must admit that our five gave but a dusty answer to questions of a political or ethical nature: how we should live, what kind of society or government we should have. Freud's austere scientism forebade him from prescribing solutions: here is the knowledge, he said, use it as you will or ignore it at your peril; I am no prophet or politician. Freud undercuts the avid political reformer or activist by suggesting that his zeal springs from some inner turmoil, some personal unhappiness. We psychoanalyze revolutionaries and world-changers to discover the neurotic roots of their power fantasies. The mature person in Freud's view is beyond this sort of infantilism. She looks on the imperfect world with stoic indifference, hoping only faintly for the slow advance of reason.

Einstein had a penchant for political nostrums like world government, but his notions were extremely simplistic. He was almost a caricature of the ineffectual intellectual in politics who cannot relate to the real world but only spouts slogans and moralizes. What he said about war and capitalism and intolerance is in any case totally unoriginal, if unexceptional, and better said by others—in general, the detritus of Enlightenment utopianism. Einstein as political sage is an embarrassment. The intelligence which cut through a myriad details to formulate magnificent generalizations in physical science when applied to human affairs produced only vapid generalities. Politics is not a generalizing science like physics. There is no grand theory of politics, as Hannah Arendt, another great sage of this era, showed.

Joyce and Wittgenstein disdained the messy realm of politics for the most part. It is true that one may fish out a group of political attitudes, rather vague and inconsistent, from their words and deeds, but this was not their main interest. Wittgenstein's heroic service in World War I, his willingness to serve as a medical aide in World War II, his interest in monasticism, his work as a village schoolteacher suggest an intense yearning to attach himself to some worthy cause, but he never found one. Instead he cultivated the lonely domain of pure thought.

Joyce was so preoccupied with his art that he seems almost to have ignored the wars, the revolutions, the depressions—well worth ignoring, he doubtless thought. Near the end of his life as war approached he expressed, to Nora's disgust, a vague sympathy for Hitler.[2] Such views were flavored with an Irishman's dislike of England, perhaps. In any event, politics was hardly Joyce's forte. Charles Covell, in *The Redefinition of Conservatism*, placed Wittgenstein in the right-wing camp, but this judgment is debatable; it is better to say that the philosopher had a kind of magnificent disdain for all utopian simplicities, most but not all of which happen to be found on the Left.

Sartre was another story, but in the end his forays into the realm of the practical came to little. That he was so widely looked to by the young indicates how much need there was and is for intellectual guidance. But he showed all the "incredible blindness," in the words of Gabriel Marcel, of the intellectual in politics. Neither Soviet Communism nor New Left radicalism came close to being a realistic program for the West, or indeed for the world in general. Sartre tried to break out of the intellectuals' inability to make effective contact with the real world. Sartre, like Joyce, showed a good deal of impatience with the impotent, irresponsible intellectual, imprisoned in a world of words and ideas, paralyzed for action by ultrasensitivity. It was a condition he loathed, partly a self-loathing (consider Mathieu, Sartre's alter ego, in *The Age of Reason*), but which in the end he could not escape. He ended in political absurdity and isolation, leader of a small clique of people totally alienated from the mainstream of social life. Like Bertrand Russell's, Sartre's temperament was marred by all the defects one can possibly imagine in a politician, including rage, the moralizing of every issue, hurling of insults at all who disagreed with him, extremism, a perfectionism refusing all compromise, rushing into sensational allegations in advance of full knowledge, attribution of base motives to foes. Such antics delighted a small number of uncritical adherents but precluded any appeal to the vast majority. Sartre himself was not happy with these personal tendencies.[3]

Integrity was perhaps our writers' highest virtue. To say they were "selfless in their pursuit of truth" is a statement that would invite a scepticism they themselves have taught us: writing, thought, and intellectual mastery is a form of desire and will to power. They all wanted to conquer the world and make themselves in some sense the king of it. If we want to achieve fame, immortality, success in life, what better models to follow than these men, whose names and books are still alive and probably always will be as long as civilization exists? But there is much truth, too, in the statement that they sought truth above all else. All of our group dedicated their lives in effect to nothing else but this. They all spurned worldly goods as a goal of life. Their tastes were simple. Einstein's carelessness of dress and Wittgenstein's scorn for idle amusements spring to mind, but even the worldlier Sartre bought one suit every year and wore it every day. Their happy lives came from the pleasures of the mind. If Freud enjoyed music less than the others,[4] he had his collection of classical antiquities and love of mountain climbing. Travel and exploration appealed to all of them, Sartre and Wittgenstein perhaps the most. Richard Ellmann says that "Joyce was traveller by nature as well as necessity."

None of these titans spent much time in the company of the others. Brief connections between them are fascinatingly numerous, more than we have space to list. Earlier we referred to the chance meeting between Freud and Einstein. Joyce initially like Freud wanted to attend medical school but had to abandon the plan seemingly for want of funds. Can we imagine the author of that supreme dream analysis *Finnegans Wake* as a psychotherapist? Joyce liked to point out that his name means the same thing in English as Freud's does in German. In 1927 Einstein, who had never met Joyce, signed a petition protesting against an American publisher's pirating of *Ulysses*. We find the lives and deeds of these men intersecting with regularity in the course of the twentieth century. In the end we must get what we can from these and other careers of genius. If we like, we can profit as much by avoiding their faults as by imitating their virtues. Examining their personal relations, we can assemble a considerable catalog of these foibles. It is fair to say that all of them revealed a certain ruthlessness in exploiting others, which they justified by the superiority of the artist's rights. Freud's patient Martha tended his home and raised his children only to be rather deserted by him in his later years as he leaned on his daughter Anna. The scenario, reminiscent of *Finnegans Wake*, repeated itself with variations in the cases of Sartre and Beauvoir, Einstein and Maric.

But of course it is not because they lived exemplary lives that we celebrate these men. What counts is their art. Did they bequeath to the century soon to begin a rich and powerful legacy of hard-won truths, insights, and values? Or did they only register the decadence of our too-old, too-sceptical civilization? That we do not yet know.

Notes

[1] See on this point Henry Staten, *Wittgenstein and Derrida* (1984); Christina Howells, "Sartre and Derrida," *Journal of the British Society for Phenomenology* (January 1982).

[2] "Joyce, although not as outspokenly pro-German as he had been during the First World War, never denounced Hitler in the ringing terms that many of his later admirers might have wished. . . . Of Hitler he once said scornfully, "Give him Europe!" Insensitively, one night at the Léons he remarked how impressed he was with Hitler's immense force and powers of leadership. [Joyce's friend Paul Léon was Jewish and subsequently murdered by the Nazis.] That was too much for Nora." (quoted in Brenda Maddox, *Nora*, pp. 332–33). Yet in general Joyce was notably pro-Jewish, as the sympathetic portrait of Leopold Bloom indicates.

[3] Sartre's biographer says that "[his] life was less a pilgrimage towards the truth than a series of intellectual and political adventures in which he strenuously entangled himself in self-deception and angrily extricated himself." Ronald Hayman, *Writing Against: A Biography of Sartre* (1986), p. 446.

[4] Einstein's violin and Wittgenstein's clarinet could have joined Sartre's piano and Joyce's fine tenor voice to make a nice quartet. Music was deeply important to all of them; no key to *Finnegans Wake* can overlook the inclusion of scores of operatic arias and names of singers, especially tenors.

Bibliography

FREUD

The Standard Edition of the Complete Psychological Works of Sigmund Freud, translated chiefly by James Strachey, was published by Hogarth Press, 1953–74, in twenty-three volumes. A selection, *Basic Writings*, ed. A. A. Brill, was published in 1938. More recently the Pelican Freud Library has printed Freud's major works in fourteen Penguin paperbacks. There are many other editions of these celebrated works, especially *The Interpretation of Dreams* (8th ed., 1954; Freud revised and added voluminously to this book over the years), *Studies in Sexuality, Case Histories, Totem and Taboo, The Ego and the Id*, and *Civilization and Its Discontents*. *Why War?*, written with Albert Einstein in 1933, was a League of Nations publication. Postmortem cullings from Freud included an unfinished psychobiography of President Woodrow Wilson, coauthored with American diplomat William Bullitt, not generally regarded as one of Freud's more successful enterprises; and *The Cocaine Papers*, from Freud's early experiments in therapeutic uses of that drug, which he abandoned upon discovering it to be addictive.

There have been some complaints about the Standard Edition translation, or about the impossibility of translating Freud at all (see e.g. Bruno Bettelheim, *Freud and Man's Soul* [1983]), but others, while admitting that Strachey and Ernest Jones subtly altered Freud in the direction of a scientific positivism, think their translation most serviceable. See Meira Likierman, "Re-translating Freud," *TLS*, July 7–13, 1989, and subsequent response from Paul Roazen.

Note: Only books in English are included in this listing.

The expiration of the copyright to Freud's writings in September 1989 may stimulate fresh translations.

More of Freud's writings keep bobbing up, the abundant letters are scattered in numerous places, and there is need for a new complete English edition. The German-language public is better served. Disarray in the the Freud Archives in London, administered by his daughter Anna until her death in 1982, seems to have been a factor in delaying a definitive edition of Freud in English; see Janet Malcolm, *In the Freud Archives* (1986). Only a few years ago the revealing correspondence between Freud and Wilhelm Fliess was finally published, edited by Jeffrey Moussaieff Masson (1985). Masson then (predictably) seceded from the organization amid bitter recriminations and wrote an anti-Freud book published in 1984.

For a list of Freud's published books see the "Freud" entry in Elizabeth Devine, et al., eds., *Thinkers of the Twentieth Century* (1984), pp. 178–81. Ronald W. Clark, *Freud, the Man and the Cause* (1980) updated Ernest Jones's account of his master's life, *Life and Work of Sigmund Freud* (3 vols., 1953–55), a valuable work flawed by its author's deeply emotional involvement in the power struggles of Freud's entourage. A number of other recent works add to an understanding of Freud's life, among them notably Peter Gay, *Freud: A Life for Our Time* (1988); Bella Zonuso, *The Young Freud* (1986); W. J. McGrath, *Freud's Discovery of Psychoanalysis* (1986); Mark Kanzer and Jules Glenn, ed., *Freud and His Patients* (1980). Elisabeth Young-Bruehl's biography of *Anna Freud* (1989) sheds some fascinating light on the Freudian enlarged family despite being rather hagiographical. Muriel Gardiner, *The Wolf-Man and Sigmund Freud* and Phillip McCaffrey, *Freud and Dora: The Artful Dream* (1984)—cf. Hannah Decker, "Freud and Dora," *Journal of Social History* (Spring 1981)—are examples of detailed, critical accounts of Freud's famous cases, which allegedly he sometimes reported with less than total accuracy; cf. François Roustang, *Psychoanalysis Never Lets Go* (1983), also Joseph Frank, "Freud's Case History of Dostoevsky," *TLS*, July 18, 1975. Marie Balmary, *Psychoanalyzing Psychoanalysis* (1982) probes Freud's own case history as a source of his personality. See also Alexander Grinstein, *Sigmund Freud's Dreams* (1968, rev. ed. 1980).

As is the case with all our figures, there is literally no end to such writings about Freud. A reviewer (*TLS*, Jan. 3, 1986) remarked that despite Freud's obvious importance "it is hard to justify the recent flood of books on the subject." That the literature on Freud is probably even larger than that on any of the others of our group may be not only because he touches so many intellectual territories (psychology, philosophy, the arts, literature, popular culture, religion) but also because he is a figure who invites ideological and methodological polemics. The sound of axes being ground is heard so loudly that by comparison the others, even Sartre, are almost noncontroversial. Violent critiques are represented by H. J. Eysenck, *Decline and Fall of the Freudian Empire* (1985), as well as his (with Glenn D. Wilson) *Experimental Study of Freudian Theories* (1972); both books are from a behavioralist perspective. David Stannard, *Shrinking History: On Freud and the Failure of Psychohistory* (1980) has a self-explanatory thesis. Polemical too is Adolf Grunbaum, *The Foundations of Psychoanalysis: A Philosophical Critique* (1985). Sara Kofman, *The Enigma of Woman: Women in Freud's Writings* (1985), is more subtle than some feminist attacks on Freud. More judicious appraisals are B. A. Farrell, *The Standing of Psychoanalysis* (1981), Marthe Robert, *The Psychoanalytic Revolution* (tr. 1966), Marshall Edelson, *Psychoanalysis—A Theory in Crisis* (1988), and Erich Fromm, *The Crisis of Psychoanalysis* (1970).

Exploring Freud's relationship to a variety of fields are such books as Ian Craib, *Psychoanalysis and Social Theory* (1989); Edwin R. Wallace, *Freud's Anthropology* (1983); Steven Marcus, *Freud and the Culture of Psychoanalysis* (1984); Harry Trossman, *Freud and the Imaginative World* (1985); Lionel Trilling, "Freud and Literature" in *The Liberal Imagination* (1950); Frederick Hoffman, *Freudianism and the Literary Mind* (1957); Richard Wollheim, ed., *Philosophers on Freud* (1977); Gerald N. Izenberg, *The Crisis of Autonomy: The Existentialist Critique of Freud* (1976); Stan Draenos, *Freud's Odyssey* (1982). Paul Roazen, *Freud and His Followers* (1971) covered most of the disciples and offshoots though not to Anna Freud's satisfaction. Consult also Edith Kurzweil, *The Freudians* (1989). Freud's early associates and disciples have all received scholarly treatment, as in E. James Lieberman, *Acts of Will: Life and Work of Otto Rank* (1985); Carl M. and Sylvia Grossman, *The Wild Analyst: The Life and Works of Georg Groddeck* (1965); Robert S. Steele, *Freud and Jung* (1982) and Walter Kaufmann, *Freud versus Adler and Jung* (1980), also *The Freud-Jung Letters* (1974); and Phyllis Grosskurth, *Melanie Klein, Her World and Her Work* (1986). Judith M. Hughes, *Reshaping the Psychoanalytic Domain* (1989) features the important British school based on but significantly revising Freud: Klein, Fairbairn, Winnicott. Sherry Turkle, *Psychoanalytic Politics: Freud's French Revolution* (1978) deals with the neo-Freudian revival under Jacques Lacan's influence in postwar France. Richard King, *The Party of Eros* (1972) and Paul Robinson, *The Freudian Left* (1969) described the politically radical offshoot that featured Wilhelm Reich and Herbert Marcuse. Arnold Goldberg, ed., *The Future of Psychoanalysis: Essays in Honor of Heinz Kohut* (1983) appraised the state of the art. Benjamin Nelson, ed., *Freud and the Twentieth Century* (1957) and Jonathan Miller, ed., *Freud: The Man, His World, His Influence* (1972) are among books that tried to survey Freud's immense influence.

A documentary film about Freud was made in the 1920s; for the film *Freud* directed by John Huston and released in 1962, Jean-Paul Sartre wrote the script (see below in Sartre bibliography), a rather fanciful one that converted Bertha Pappenheim into a compulsive prostitute.

Not only *Philosopher's Index* and the *Isis* history of science bibliographies but *Bibliography of the History of Medicine* (National Library of Medicine, Washington, D.C.) can supply help in finding the numerous additional sources.

EINSTEIN

As is the case with each of our other figures, the attempt to assemble and publish all of Einstein's writings bears a trace of scandal. Einstein died in 1955. After years of preliminary maneuvering (the project was first proposed in 1975), Volume 1 of *The Collected Papers of Albert Einstein* came from Princeton University Press in 1987, covering the years from 1879 to 1902 (ed. John Stachel; English translation in a separate volume). Vol. 2, *The Swiss Years: Writings 1900–1909* appeared in 1989. They will be followed by many more, the publication dates reaching no doubt well into the next century, providing a richly detailed source of information about Einstein. That the writings of the century's greatest scientist waited so long for definitive publication stemmed in good part from obstacles posed by the executor of Einstein's estate, Otto Nathan. The project is lavishly endowed, yet some critics found the vol. 1 research disappointing from a historical point of view. (See, e.g., Lewis Pyenson's review in *Isis*, March 1989.) The juiciest part was some previously unpublished letters between Einstein and his first wife Mileva Maric revealing among other things the out-of-wedlock birth of their first child. (Questions about the role of Maric were taken up by feminists, for it appears that she may have contributed much more to him not only personally but scientifically than she has usually been given credit for.) As this grand editing project continues and (it is hoped) improves, we will learn much more about Einstein's life than we now know (or perhaps need to know). Meanwhile some of Einstein's writings were collected in *The World As I See It* (1934) and *Out of My Later Years* (1950), which included his ruminations on war, peace, world government, socialism, etc., as well as on science and philosophy. *Einstein on Peace* (1960) was edited by Otto Nathan and Heinz Norden. His lectures in 1921 on *The Meaning of Relativity* were in their fourth edition by 1953. The recently published *Ideas and Opinions* is culled mostly from the latter four books.

Previous biographies in English, only partly satisfactory, were Ronald W. Clark, *Einstein: Life and Times* (1971) and Abraham Pais, *"Subtle is the Lord": The Science and Life of Albert Einstein* (1984). Banesh Hoffmann, *Albert Einstein: Creator and Rebel* (1972) is by a friend and colleague, author also of *The Strange Story of the Quantum* (1959).

The Genesis of Relativity, by L. S. Swenson (1979) treats a fascinating subject also handled capably in Lewis Pyenson, *The Young Einstein: The Advent of Relativity* (1985); Elie Zahar, *Einstein's Revolution: A Study in Heuristic* (1989);

Russell McCormmach, ed., *Historical Studies in the Physical Sciences,* (especially valuable is vol. 7 [1976], which has articles by Pyenson, Stanley Goldberg, and Tetu Hirosige); Arthur I. Miller, *Einstein's Special Theory of Relativity: Emergence and Early Interpretation* (1981); see also his *Frontiers of Physics, 1900–1911* (1986). Christa Jungnickel and Russell McCormmach, *Intellectual Mastery of Nature: Theoretical Physics from Ohm to Einstein* (2 vols., 1986) is a magisterial survey. Stephen Kern, *The Culture of Space and Time, 1880–1918* (1983); P. M. Herman, *Energy, Force and Matter: The Development of Nineteenth Century Physics* (1982); Jed Z. Buchwald, *From Maxwell to Microphysics* (1985) are all valuable. The first of a series of *Einstein Studies* announced by Birkäuser, Boston, was Don Howard and John Stachel, ed., *Einstein and the History of General Relativity* (1989), proceedings of a 1986 conference. L. Pearce Williams, ed., *Relativity Theory: Its Origins and Impact on Modern Thought* (1968) is still useful as an introduction to Einstein's influence. Lewis S. Feuer's *Einstein and the Generations of Science* (1982) is an interesting psychosocial approach; cf. the well-known *Structure of Scientific Revolutions* by Thomas S. Kuhn (1962).

The many efforts to explain Einstein's relativity theories in more or less ordinary language—an inherently impossible task, many think—are perhaps best represented by Bertrand Russell, *The ABC of Relativity* (1959), Lincoln Barnett, *The Universe and Dr. Einstein* (1964), Nigel Calder, *Einstein's Universe* (1979), and Stanley Goldberg, *Understanding Relativity* (1984). Einstein himself wrote a popular explanation, *Relativity,* first published in 1916, as well as *The Meaning of Relativity.* See also Isaac Azimov's *Understanding Physics: The Electron, Proton, and Neutron* (1966), and Robert M. Wald, *Space, Time, and Gravity* (1977), an accessible scientific summary of the General Relativity theory. Arthur Fine, *The Shaky Game: Einstein, Realism, and the Quantum Theory* (1986) gives a good account of this notable debate. Michio Kaku and Jennifer Trainer, *Beyond Einstein: The Cosmic Quest for the Theory of the Universe* (1987) is about recent reformulations of Einstein's unified field theory. James S. Trefil, *From Atoms to Quarks: An Introduction to the Strange World of Particle Physics* (1981) is good. On modern physics and the occult: Fred Alan Wolf, *Star Wave: Mind, Consciousness, and Quantum Physics* (1985).

Works like Arthur Eddington, *The Philosophy of Physical Science* (1939), James Jeans, *Physics and Philosophy* (1942), and Milic Capek, *The Philosophical Impact of Modern Physics* (1961) led on to many other discussions among philosophers relating to space, time, the mind and physical reality which still go on at a great rate. For a discussion see "Science vs. Reality: A Debate," *Dalhousie Review* (Fall 1984). Alan J. Friedman and Carol C. Donley, *Einstein As Myth and Muse* (1985) offers something on this subject, but much more is needed to document the great scientist's impact on general culture.

There are good recent studies of a host of Einstein's fellow scientists with whom he interacted in so many ways, among them Planck, Lorentz, Rutherford, Bohr, Dirac, Schrödinger, Broglie, Heisenberg, Hahn, and Meitner. For aid in finding books and articles on all history of science subjects, consult the annual bibliographies of the journal *Isis* (*Cumulative Bibliography 1966–75*, 2 vols., 1980; 1976–85, 2 vols., 1989).

WITTGENSTEIN

Wittgenstein published only one book in his lifetime, the famous albeit brief *Tractatus Logico-Philosophicus* (translated from the German; London: Kegan Paul, Trench, Trubner & Co., 1922; later editions from Routledge & Kegan Paul); plus one article (1929) and a short review (1913)! Published in 1953 not long after his death, *Philosophical Investigations* (Oxford: Basil Blackwell) was based on material dictated at Cambridge between 1933 and 1935. Later *The Blue and Brown Books*, the basis of *Philosophical Investigations*, was published separately in 1964 by Blackwell, as were (1961–1980) a number of other volumes derived from Wittgenstein's letters, notes, dictations, and conversations: *Notebooks, 1914–16*; *Letters to Russell, Keynes, and Moore*; *Zettel* (clippings); *Philosophical Remarks*; *Remarks on the Foundations of Mathematics*; *Culture and Value*; *Lectures and Conversations on Aesthetics, Psychology and Religious Belief*; *Remarks on the Philosophy of Psychology* (2 vols.), and (from University of Chicago Press, 1988), *Wittgenstein's Lectures on Philosophical Psychology, 1946–47* (psychology was Wittgenstein's preoccupation from about 1946 to 1949). The man who once said it was necessary to be silent had obviously not lived up to this prescription. *A Wittgenstein Bibliography* was edited by V. A. and S. G. Shanker as vol. 5 of a series, *Ludwig Wittgenstein: Critical Assessments* (1987).

There is evidently a good deal more Wittgenstein *Nachlass*, but his literary executor, G. H. von Wright, who edited the above volumes, said that "all the works of major interest" had been published by 1980. Others think the yet unpublished (though available on microfilm) notebooks are valuable; see Jaakko Hintikka, "Obstacles to Understanding," *TLS*, Sept. 28-Oct. 4, 1990. A systematic effort to bring all of his papers together at Wren Library, Trinity College, Cambridge, began in 1969. A complete edition of his works remains to be published despite some aborted attempts. Wright's *Wittgenstein* (1982) tells much of this publication history. For the general reader a useful selection is Gerd Brand, ed., *The Central Texts of Ludwig Wittgenstein* (1979), published in the United States as *The Essential Wittgenstein*.

As with all our figures, the secondary literature is too vast to do more than sample. The leading biography is being written by Brian McGuinness; *Wittgenstein: A Life*; vol. 1, *Young Ludwig, 1889–1921* appeared in 1988. See also McGuiness, ed., *Wittgenstein and His Times* (1982). A notable attempt to relate the philosopher to his environment was Alan Janik and Stephen Toulmin's *Wittgenstein's Vienna* (1973). An article by Peter C. John, "Wittgenstein's 'Wonderful Life,'" *Journal of the History of Ideas* (July–Sept. 1988) is evocative and sensitive. A more controversial study is W. W. Bartley III, *Wittgenstein* (rev. ed. 1985). See also a new biography entitled *Ludwig Wittgenstein: The Duty of Genius* (1990) by Ray Monk.

P. M. S. Hacker, *Insight and Illusion: Themes in the Philosophy of Wittgenstein* (1987), a revision of a book published in 1972 with the same title, has been called the best general study of Wittgenstein's thought. With G. P. Baker, Hacker has also written *Wittgenstein: Meaning and Understanding. Essays on the "Philosopical Investigations"* (1983). Norman Malcolm, *Nothing Is Hidden: Wittgenstein's Criticism of His Early Thought* (1987) comes from a distinguished student of Wittgenstein. A less sympathetic account by a famous philosopher is A. J. Ayer's *Wittgenstein* (1985). David Pears offered a brief, perceptive introduction in the Fontana Modern Masters series (1971), and wrote the more detailed *The False Prison: A Study of the Development of Wittgenstein's Philosophy* (vol. 1, 1987). See also Anthony Kenny, *Wittgenstein* (1973) and *The Legacy of Wittgenstein* (1986); A. C. Grayling, *Wittgenstein* (1988); Saul A. Kripke, *Wittgenstein on Rules and Private Language* (1983); S. Stephen Hilmy, *The Later Wittgenstein* (1987); Stanley Cavell, *The Claim of Reason: Wittgenstein, Skepticism, Morality, and Tragedy* (1979).

A book which connects Wittgenstein to others of our group is Morris Lazerowitz, *The Language of Philosophy: Freud and Wittgenstein* (1977). Other interesting connections: Henry Staten, *Wittgenstein and Derrida* (1984); an essay on Hegel and Wittgenstein in David Lamb, ed., *Hegel and Modern Philosophy* (1987); David Rubinstein, *Marx and Wittgenstein* (1981), also Susan Easton, *Humanist Marxism and Wittgensteinian Social Philosophy* (1983)—rather unconvincing exercises which should not obscure Wittgenstein's essentially conservative political outlook, as most see it; Friedrich Waismann, *Wittgenstein and the Vienna Circle* (1979); Gordon Baker, *Wittgenstein, Frege, and the Vienna Circle* (1988); Jorn K. Braman, *Wittgenstein's 'Tractatus' and the Modern Arts* (1985); John W. Danford, *Wittgenstein and Political Philosophy* (1978); Malcolm Budd, *Wittgenstein's Philosophy of Psychology* (1989); Hannah F. Pitkin, *Wittgenstein and Justice* (1975); Aryeh Botwinick, *Wittgenstein and Historical Understanding* (1981). Thomas D. Peterson, *Wittgenstein for Preaching* (1980) seeks to bring Wittgenstein into "humble daily use," which he surely would have liked. Peter Winch's *Simone Weil* explores an affinity between Wittgenstein and the passionate Jewish-French mystic. Consult also Glen T. Martin, *From Nietzsche to Wittgenstein: The Problem of Truth and Nihilism in the Modern World* (1989). Also of interest is Roy Harris, *Language, Saussure, and Wittgenstein: How to Play Games with Words* (1990). Helpful in finding further books and articles is *Philosopher's Index*, published annually.

JOYCE

The text of *Ulysses* is still in fearful controversy. In 1986 Random House hit the best-seller list with a new and presumably definitive edition, edited by Hans Walter Gabler with Wolfhard Steppe and Claus Melchior (earlier, 1984, published in 3 volumes by Garland Press). Though it carried the endorsement of the dean of Joyce scholars, the late Richard Ellmann, and was praised as supplying important corrections to the old edition, it was soon assailed as defective, with the even more damning insinuation that the new edition had been rushed into print to prolong the about-to-expire copyright. (The first Random House edition was published in 1934.) See John Kidd's "The Scandal of Ulysses," *New York Review of Books*, June 30, 1988; reply from Gabler in *NYRB*, August 18, 1988; correspondence in *TLS*, July 22–28, 1988, from Prof. Kidd, and Sept. 2–8, 1988, from Prof. Charles Rossman; also *Assessing the 1984 "Ulysses"*, ed. George Sandulescu and Clive Hart (1986). Perhaps, as many have thought, an exactly "correct" text is impossible because Joyce changed his mind so often, constantly fiddling with his words (to do so obviously being of his very nature). And if *Ulysses* was a typesetter's nightmare, what of *Finnegans Wake!* The 1939 edition published by Viking Press and Faber & Faber seems unlikely to be replaced for a while yet. The multivolumed *James Joyce Archives*, ed. Michael Groden, et al. (1978) printed drafts and proofs of both *Ulysses* and *Finnegans Wake*. Viking Press has published critical editions of Joyce's other writings, which tend to get overlooked amid the excitement of his two blockbusters: *Collected Poems, Dubliners, Exiles, Critical Writings* (ed. Ellmann and E. Mason, 1959), *Portrait of the Artist*, and of course the letters.

Materials relating to Joyce's private life are equally in the combat zone, similar to the struggles over the Freud and Sartre papers. A large number of unpublished letters and other manuscripts arrived at Cornell University in 1957 by way of the widow of James Joyce's often unaffectionate brother, Stanislaus, who had kept them largely to himself before his death in 1955 (on Bloomsday), except for showing them to biographer Ellmann in 1953. These included the explicitly erotic letters the Joyces wrote to each other when they were apart in 1909, which Ellmann avoided in his biography of 1959 but later printed, to the amazement of even those jaded by the liberated '60s and '70s (*Selected Letters*, 1975). Publishing this extremely intimate (to say the least) material deeply offended Joyce's surviving relatives, especially his grandson Stephen. The Joyces' daughter, Lucia, was in a mental institution; their son George was an alcoholic. Nora had died in 1951; Harriet Weaver, Joyce's longtime patron and guardian angel, ten years later. It was certain they would never have consented to publication of the scandalous letters, and the surviving Joyces resented it. They refused Brenda Maddox permission to use material relating to Lucia in her brilliant and sympathetic biography of Nora Joyce (*Nora: The Real Life of Molly Bloom*, 1988).

Joyce materials may be found in many libraries, in the United States notably at the university libraries of SUNY–Buffalo, Texas, and Southern Illinois in addition to Cornell. See Michael Grodon, *James Joyce's Manuscripts: An Index* (1980); Thomas Jackson Rice, *James Joyce: A Guide to Research* (1982). There are papers at the National Library of Ireland to be opened in 1991 which may include more of the steamy 1909 correspondence. These had been rescued from Joyce's apartment by Paul Léon as the Germans occupied Paris in April 1940 and deposited with the Irish embassy in Paris.

The classic biography is Ellmann's (1959; revised edition 1982), though it has been accused of distortions imposed on it by way of Stanislaus's testimony. Brenda Maddox's *Nora* must now rank as the next most informative biography. Stanislaus Joyce's *My Brother's Keeper* (1958) may be slanted but is wonderfully illuminating at times. So is Joyce's friend Frank Budgen's *James Joyce and the Making of Ulysses* (1960).

Guidance to the manifold other sources for Joyce's life, as well as his work, may be found in such reference books as Zack Bowen and James C. Carens, *A Companion to Joyce Studies* (1984); Robert H. Deming, *A Bibliography of Joyce Studies* (1977); above all, in the pages of *The James Joyce Quarterly* which has been the industry's chief periodical since 1963. It is notably assisted by the bimonthly *Newslitter* (*sic*; finneganese) which keeps up with the hundreds of suggested readings of the *Wake*; also by the *James Joyce Broadsheet* (London).

A selection from the vast Joyce industry: Colin McCabe, *James Joyce and the Revolution of the Word* (1979); Richard Ellmann, *The Consciousness of Joyce* (1977); Suzette A. Henke, *Joyce's Moraculous Sindbook: A Study of "Ulysses"* (1978); Hugh Kenner, *Ulysses* (rev. ed., 1987); Mark Schechner, *Joyce in Night-town: A Psychoanalytical Inquiry into Ulysses* (1974). Indispensable guides to the mysteries of the *Wake* are Joseph Campbell and Henry Morton Robinson, *A Skeleton Key to Finnegans Wake* (1944); Roland McHugh, *Annotations to Finnegans Wake* (1980) and *The Finnegans Wake Experience* (1982); William Y. Tindall, *A Reader's Guide to Finnegans Wake* (1969); Clive Hart, *Structure and Motif in Finnegans Wake* (1962); John Bishop, *Joyces's Book of the Dead* (1986); Bernard Benstock, *Joyce-Again's Wake* (1965). Among a large number of other books and articles tracking down *Wake* allusions are James S. Atherton, *The Books at the Wake* (1974); Louis O. Mink, *A Finnegans Wake Gazeteer* (1978); Ruth Bauerle, ed., *The James Joyce Songbook* (1983).

Works relating Joyce to other thinkers and movements: Sheldon Brivic, *Joyce between Freud and Jung* (1980); Bonnie Kime Scott, *Joyce and Feminism* (1984); B. J. Tysdahl, *Joyce and Ibsen* (1968); Donald Phillip Verene, ed., *Vico and Joyce* (1986); Mary T. Reynolds, *Joyce and Dante: The Shaping Imagination* (1987);

Umberto Eco, *The Aesthetics of Chaosmos: The Middle Ages of James Joyce* (tr. 1982); Richard Brown, *James Joyce and Sexuality* (Cambridge, 1985). Appraisals of the Joyce influence include Marvin Magalaner and Richard M. Kain, *Joyce: The Man, the Work, the Reputation* (1957); Robert M. Adams, *Afterjoyce: Studies in Fiction after Ulysses* (1977); David Hayman and Elliott Anderson, ed., *In the Wake of the Wake* (1978); Heyward Ehrlich, ed., *Light Rays: James Joyce and Modernism* (1984).

Movies: *Ulysses* (1967), predictably not very successful; "Fionnula Flanagan as 'James Joyce's Women'" (1987), filming of a celebrated stage performance; "The Dead," from a Joyce story (1988).

SARTRE

The state of Sartre's writings is rather like that of Wittgenstein's a decade ago: no definitive total edition yet, attempts to establish a single manuscript repository (in the *Bibliothèque Nationale*), continuing posthumous publication of miscellaneous leftovers. Unlike Wittgenstein, of course, Sartre published voluminously in his lifetime. His chief philosophical works, *Being and Nothingness* (tr. 1956) and *The Critique of Dialectical Reason* remain available in English translation as do collections of shorter pieces, *Existentialism and Humanism* (1948), *What is Literature?* (1949, 1988), *Politics and Literature* (1973), *Literary and Philosophical Essays* (1955), *Baudelaire* (1949), *Psychology of Imagination: Sartre on Theater* (1976). The novels in English translation include *Nausea* and the three completed novels of the *Roads to Freedom* (*Les chemins de la liberté*, 1945–49): *The Age of Reason, Iron in the Soul,* and *The Reprieve. Sartre in the Seventies: Interviews and Essays* was published in London in 1978. His autobiographical *Les mots* was translated as *The Words* (1964), and the huge unfinished Flaubert biography as *The Family Idiot* in an edition slowly emerging from the University of Chicago Press, to reach five volumes when completed (the first volume, 1982, received some criticism for the translation. Vol. 3 appeared in 1990). See also *Saint Genet, Actor and Martyr* (1963, 1983); *Mallarmé or the Poet of Nothingness* (1988). Most of Sartre's plays are available in translation (*The Flies, No Exit, The Condemned of Altona,* and others.) *The War Diaries* (1985) and *The Freud Scenario* (1986) have appeared since his death. Other posthumous publications in France have not thus far been translated, e.g. *Verité et existence*, ed. Arlette Elkaim-Sartre (1989). Simone's *Lettres à Sartre* was published in Paris in 1990 (2 vols.) as well as her wartime journal (1939–41), edited by Sylvie Le Bon-de Beauvoir. Rivalry between Sylvie and Arlette will complicate but doubtless spice this ongoing release of Sartre material.

Biographies of Sartre include Annie Cohen-Solal, *Sartre: A Biography* (1987); Ronald Hayman, *Writing Against: A Biography of Sartre* (1986); John

Gerassi, *Sartre: Hated Conscience of His Time,* vol. 1 (1989). Valuable both for life and work is Paul Schilpp, ed., *The Philosophy of Jean-Paul Sartre* (1981); one paper in it compares Sartre and Freud. Howard Davies, *Sartre and "Les Temps Modernes"* (1987) documents an important part of Sartre's career. Of course, Simone de Beauvoir's life and work are almost inseparable from Sartre's; *Memoirs of a Dutiful Daughter, The Prime of Life, Force of Circumstance, All Said and Done,* her earlier autobiographical writings spanning the years from 1958 to 1974), were climaxed by her farewell tribute to Sartre, *Le cérémonie des adieux,* translated as *Adieux: Farewell to Sartre* (1984). Works on Beauvoir include Mary Evans, *Simone de Beauvoir, a Feminist Mandarin* (1985); Terry Keefe, *Simone de Beauvoir: A Study of Her Writings* (1983); Axel Madsen, *Hearts and Minds: The Common Journey of Simone de Beauvoir and Jean-Paul Sartre* (1977); Deirdre Bair, *Simone de Beauvoir: A Biography* (1990). The definitive biography is probably yet to come when all the documents are available, though Bair has used many of them.

Raymond Aron's *Memoires* (1983) contain much of interest about Sartre. Telling criticism of Sartre's "ultra-bolshevism" of the early '50s came from his one-time friend and fellow existentialist Maurice Merleau-Ponty in *Adventures of the Dialectic* (1973). Claude Levi-Strauss notably criticized his historical methods from a structuralist point of view in *The Savage Mind* (1966).

Studies of Sartre's thought, large and small, are, again, almost bewilderingly abundant. A selection: Istvan Meszaros, *The Work of Sartre* (vol. 1, 1979); Peter Caws, *Sartre* (1979); Arthur C. Danto, *Sartre* (Fontana Modern Masters, 1975); Dominick LaCapra, *A Preface to Sartre* (1988), a Derridean interpretation; Christina Howells, *Sartre: The Necessity of Freedom* (1988), in the series "Major European Authors" from Cambridge University Press; Germaine Bree, *Camus and Sartre* (1972); Joseph Fell, *Heidegger and Sartre* (1979); Mark Poster, *Existential Marxism in Postwar France* (1976); Raymond Aron, *History and the Dialectic of Violence: An Analysis of Sartre's Critique* (1973); Ronald Aronson, *Sartre's Second Critique* (1987); Thomas R. Flynn, *Sartre and Marxist Existentialism* (1986); Gila J. Hayim, *The Existentialist Sociology of Jean-Paul Sartre* (1980); Betty Cannon, *Sartre and Psychoanalysis* (1990); Hazel Barnes, *Sartre and Flaubert* (1981); Michael Scriven, *Sartre's Existential Biographies* (1984); Rhiannon Goldthorpe, *Sartre: Literature Theory* (1984); Betty T. Rahv, *From Sartre to the New Novel* (1974); William Plank, *Sartre and Surrealism* (1981).

Valuable as a reference tool is F. and C. Lapointe, *Jean-Paul Sartre and His Critics: An International Bibliography, 1938–1980* (2d ed., 1981), also Michel Contat and Michel Rybalka, *The Writings of Jean-Paul Sartre* (2 vols., 1974).

With Alexandre Astruc, Contat directed a film, *Sartre by Himself* (1974).

Index

	Freud	Einstein	Wittgenstein
1900	*The Interpretation of Dreams*	graduates from Zurich Technical College	
	Three Essays on the Theory of Sexuality	publishes "On the Electrodynamics of Moving Bodies"; receives doctorate from University of Zurich resides in Prague then Zurich	Wittgenstein, aeronautics student at Manchester since 1908, begins philosophy studies at Cambridge with Bertrand Russell
1910	forms with Jung International Psychoanalytical Association		
		becomes professor of physics at University of Berlin	
	friendship with Jung breaks up; *Totem and Taboo*		works on thesis in Norway
		develops general relativity theory which is supported by worldwide observations in 1919	serves as soldier in Austrian army during World War I
1920	*Beyond the Pleasure Principle*		
		joins Zionist movement; develops unified field theory	
	The Ego and the Id (1923)		*Tractatus Logico-Philosophicus*
	The Future of an Illusion	debates Bohr and others on quantum mechanics at Solvay conference	returns to philosophy after a withdrawal of several years
1930	*Civilization and Its Discontents*		
	Nazis come to power		
	Freud flees from Vienna after Nazi takeover of Austria	renounces German citizenship after Nazi takeover and remains abroad	develops second philosophy at Oxford
	Freud dies in London	writes letter to President Roosevelt on need for development of atomic bomb	obtains chair of philosophy at Cambridge
1940			works as medical orderly during World War II
			interest in psychology
1950			death of Wittgenstein; posthumous publication of *Philosophical Investigations*
		death of Einstein	
1960			
1970			
1980			

128

Joyce	Sartre
1900	
graduates from University College, Dublin; settles in Trieste after leaving Dublin	Jean-Paul Sartre born June 2, 1905
1910	
publishes *Dubliners*	
publishes *Portrait of the Artist as a Young Man*; moves to Zurich	
1920 moves to Paris	
publication of *Ulysses*	
	studies at Ecole Normale Superieure with Simone de Beauvoir
excerpts from "Work in Progress" appear in *transition*	
1930	
marries Nora Barnacle	
	Sartre studies philosophy of Heidegger and Husserl in Berlin
	publication of *Nausea*
publication of *Finnegans Wake*	
1940	
death of Joyce in Zurich	
	joins Resistance; writes key existentialist works: *Being and Nothingness, The Flies, No Exit*
	Roads to Liberty novels; Beauvoir writes *The Second Sex*
1950	
	close association with Communists ends after suppression of Hungarian revolt
	writes *Critique of Dialectical Reason, Condemned of Altona*; involvement with Algerian revolution; rejects Nobel Prize; spokesman during student revolts of 1968
1960	
1970	
1980	death of Sartre in Paris

Makers of Modern Culture was copyedited and proofread by Michael Kendrick. Lucy Herz was production editor. Graphic Composition, Inc. typeset the text, and the book was printed and bound by McNaughton & Gunn, Inc.

Cover design by Vito De Pinto Graphic Design.